Alexander's Great March

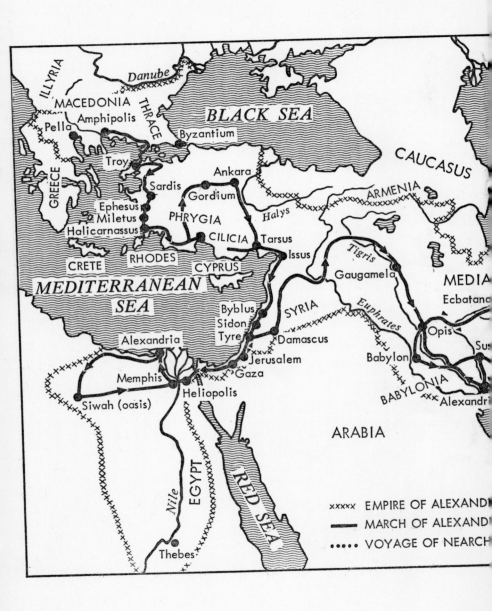

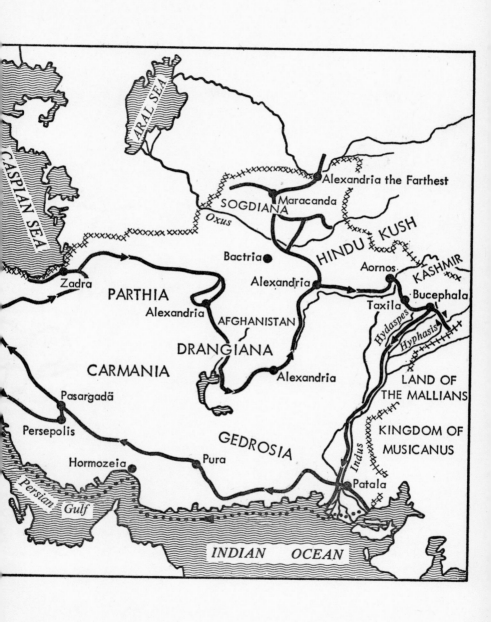

LC

Alexander's Great March

by Hans Baumann

translated by
STELLA HUMPHRIES

1968
New York
HENRY Z. WALCK, INCORPORATED

J
920
A

LIBRARY OF CONGRESS CATALOG CARD NUMBER: 68–23882
PRINTED IN THE UNITED STATES OF AMERICA

Contents

The Narrator Introduces Himself

WHEN Alexander, the young King of the Macedonians, set off on his great expedition, he had with him official pacers, whose duty it was to report to him daily what distance the army had covered in the past twenty-four hours. They were called the King's Runners and the Pace-recorders of Asia, and I was one of them.

And so it came about that I was always close to Alexander, except in battle. For we pacers were not armed, and we were no more soldiers than the scholars or the cartwright who traveled with the baggage train. It was our duty to measure every step precisely, neither adding to nor subtracting from the total. And this we did. We carried out our task scrupulously and we were praised by the King for so doing.

But there were hours when I was off duty, and then I used to collect the stories that were told in camp about Alexander. I heard them from all kinds of people, from the Companions, from his friends, from soldiers and minstrels, from Macedonians, Persians and Indians—and also from a certain poet whom I met when I returned home after the great campaign was over. He had not been present, and yet he knew more about Alexander than did we, the King's Runners.

These, then, are the tales I want to relate in this book. And just as I neither added a step nor left one out when I measured the miles we marched, so I shall tell these stories exactly as I heard them, altering nothing, even when the events are little to Alexander's credit.

It is an undisputed fact that, in the fourteen years of his reign, Alexander accomplished a feat that has no parallel in history. He conquered half the world and no one can say what might have happened, had death not struck him down at an age when most men are only at the beginning of their careers and have achieved nothing worth recording.

Yet it is not the world conqueror who is my hero in these pages. Day after day I saw Alexander, and thus I can describe what he was like as a friend and as a foe; in the hour of danger and when he held a feast; when he was roused to fury, and when he fell a prey to despair—in short what he was like as a man.

Let me speak about him now.

1

Alexander Achieves His First Victory and Learns a Secret

ALEXANDER was twelve years old when he won his first victory. Five boys of his own age were specially picked to run a race with him, and his father, King Philip, had offered a golden wreath as a prize for the winner. Alexander was the first home, a horse's length ahead of the rest of the field.

"You should enter for the laurel wreath at the next Olympic Games," said King Philip to his son.

"By all means, if I can have kings as competitors," answered Alexander. And the King was pleased with his son's reply.

King Philip was a powerful warrior. His royal capital of Pella was not fortified. "It has no need of walls, for I am there to protect it," he used to say.

He had received many wounds in battle. His left leg was as stiff as a withered branch, but on horseback he always overtook his enemies. He had only one eye, for the other had been gouged out by an arrow, yet he could see every danger that threatened, and on the battlefield he was quick to discover where victory could be found.

When messengers arrived at the royal court of Macedonia one day and announced yet another of Philip's triumphs, Alexander turned pale. Those around him were jubilant at the news and they asked him why he looked as if some disaster had befallen him. "What will be left for me to conquer, since my father has won so many battles?" he asked.

The philosopher Aristotle, who was Alexander's tutor,

told him not to worry. "The end of the world is so far away," he told him, "that no one can conquer it all by force of arms."

When Alexander heard this, his eyes flashed with excitement.

It was about this time that his mother, Queen Olympias, confided to him something that she alone knew. She was a priestess in secret, and she used to dance in temples and other holy shrines. She could hold snakes in her hands and they would not harm her. When Philip made her his wife, she dreamed that she would bear a son more glorious than all the kings on earth. And she prayed to the god who rules the world to grant her such a son. One night, she saw a streak of lightning flash from the sky and dart through her body, and she took this as a sign that her son would be divine.

Alexander was told this secret by his mother at a time when King Philip was fighting one of his wars, far away from the town of Pella.

2

Alexander Wins a Horse and Is Given a Book

THE KING of Macedonia had a passion for horses. One day, a Greek horse dealer offered to sell him a huge black charger with a snow-white blaze on its forehead, such as one often sees on cattle. That is why the horse was called Bucephalus, which means "Ox-head." The Greek wanted thirteen talents for it, which was an enormous sum of money—enough to buy five fine horses.

Everyone admired the appearance of the horse, the King included. But as soon as he tried to ride it, the beast lashed out with its hoofs, tossed its mane and danced on its hind legs. When the King's finest horseman leaped onto its back, he was thrown to the ground.

The King lost his temper. "Take the black brute out of my sight!" he roared at the horse dealer. "It's no good at all."

"Let me ride it," Alexander pleaded with his father. "It's the best horse in the world, I tell you."

"No one can ride it," said King Philip. "It will throw you too."

"If it does, I'll pay you thirteen talents," said Alexander.

Everyone laughed at the boy, and the King laid a wager with his son. Alexander went up to the horse calmly, took the bridle in his hand and turned the animal around until it was facing the sun. Now that it was no longer frightened by its own shadow, it allowed itself to be led. Alexander started whispering to the horse and it pricked up its ears. Then he quickened his steps and Bucephalus fell into a trot. A few moments later, Alexander let his riding cloak slip to the ground and he swung himself onto the horse's back. At once Bucephalus was galloping away, like a cloud scudding before the wind.

The onlookers held their breath. Not a sound could be heard but the beat of the thudding hoofs. King Philip and all those with him were anxious for the young rider's safety, but Alexander only urged Bucephalus on with words of encouragement. Sweeping around in a broad arc, he finally brought the horse to a standstill in front of the King, his father, and

5

Bucephalus did not even shy, although the whole gathering broke into shouts and cheers.

Tears of joy coursed down Philip's face. "Macedonia is too small for you, my son," he said. "You must look for another kingdom, one that is worthy of you." And he made Alexander a present of the magnificent stallion.

Alexander received another precious gift about this time. It was given to him by Aristotle, his tutor, and it was a copy of Homer's *Iliad,* the book about the Greeks who set sail for Asia to bring back Helen, the Greek queen who had been abducted by Paris, the prince of Troy. It tells of Agamemnon and Achilles, of Odysseus, Nestor, and the other Achaeans who besieged Troy for ten long years and finally conquered it with the aid of a wooden horse. Alexander read the *Iliad* every day and he yearned to visit the spot where Troy had once stood. It was there that he wanted to strike a blow against the enemies of the Greeks.

The town where Aristotle was born had been destroyed as an act of war, and when Alexander begged his father to have it rebuilt, King Philip granted his request.

The King was never tightfisted, but Alexander exceeded him in his openhanded generosity. However, only those who actually asked him for presents received them. One of his Companions was a young man called Serapion. He never asked Alexander for anything, and in consequence he never received gifts from him.

The young men were all playing a game of ball one day, and Serapion threw the ball to everyone in turn—except to Alexander. When they had finished playing, Alexander asked Serapion why he had not thrown the ball his way a single time. "I did not hear you ask me for it," replied Serapion.

Alexander had to laugh, and then and there he gave Serapion an exceptionally valuable gift.

He was most lavish on another occasion, too, when there was a ceremony of sacrifice. As the King's son, Alexander had to scatter incense over the sacred flames and he cast it on the fire in great handfuls.

One of the priests reproached him. "Only the monarch who owns the Land of Incense can be so extravagant with it," he said.

"It will be mine one day," replied Alexander, with such profound conviction that the priest was at a loss for an answer.

3

Alexander Loses His Father

SIX years later, war broke out between the Greeks and the Macedonians. The combined army of the Athenians and the Thebans assembled at Chaeronea, a solid wall of men and spears drawn up behind earthworks. The Macedonians advanced toward them, and by a cunning maneuver King Philip tricked that wall into moving. He withdrew the right flank of his army as if he were afraid, and so tempted the Athenians and the Thebans to pursue him. But as soon as the enemy had left their trenches, Philip launched an attack with his Macedonians, and the Greeks faltered. The Macedonian cavalry charged on the left, with Alexander at their head. Bucephalus streaked across the field of Chaeronea like a cloud from which lightning flashes. The wall of enemy soldiers collapsed, and the trapped armies fled.

King Philip did not have them pursued but spared the conquered. By doing so he won a far greater victory, for the Greeks chose him to be the Captain of their League. He was appointed to lead them on an expedition into Asia in order to fight the Persians whose king, Xerxes, had once desecrated Greek temples and set fire to Athens. This was a crime that Greeks would not allow to go unpunished.

But when he returned to Pella, the King caused a rift in his own household. He dismissed his queen, Olympias, and took a young princess to be his wife instead.

At the wedding feast, Alexander sat shrouded in sullen silence. King Philip drank too much. Through his befuddled haze, he saw nothing beyond the faces of the flatterers who thronged about him.

Then Attalus, the uncle of the young bride, proposed a toast to the couple and he prayed to the gods to give them a son, a legitimate heir to the throne. At such an insult, Alexander sprang to his feet and hurled a heavy goblet at the speaker's head.

This brought King Philip to his feet too. He called Alexander "the son of Olympias," as if denying that he was also his own son and heir, and he even drew his sword in an attempt to attack Alexander. But wine had been spilled on the floor and Philip was so drunk that he slipped in the puddle and could not get up again because no one would give him a hand. Then Alexander taunted him. "Look!" he cried. "This is the man who proposes to march from Europe into Asia, and he can't even get from one table to another without falling!"

That same night, Alexander fled to Illyria with his mother and his closest friends.

Soon after this, King Philip betrothed his daughter Cleopatra to a prince who was one of his allies. At the wedding ceremony, Philip was assassinated by a Macedonian whom he had offended.

4

Alexander Becomes King and Marches North

ALEXANDER at once returned home and had himself proclaimed king. The soldiers, who knew of his daring, acclaimed the nineteen-year-old prince and carried him in triumph on his shield. And Alexander lost no time in trying out the army that was now his own.

His first expedition was to the north. There in the mountains lived a tribe of brigands who were so ferocious that they were feared even by other robber bands. These mountain dwellers did not use spears but only daggers and short swords. Instead of helmets of iron or of leather, they wore foxes' skins on their heads, and they were as sly as foxes themselves. The Macedonian army advanced on them with spears and shields, and the bandits withdrew before them to heights that were almost completely inaccessible.

The brigands intended to turn the mountain valley through which Alexander advanced with his soldiers into a deadly ambush. And so they had dragged their carts up the heights on either side, and filled them with rocks and boulders. Once the Macedonians were inside the gorge these carts were sent hurtling down the mountainsides with the terrible crash of thunder.

Alexander gave orders for the Macedonians to break formation and thus allow the carts to pass through the gaps between the ranks where they could do no damage. Where there was not enough space for the soldiers to thin out in this way, they threw themselves to the ground and covered themselves with their shields. The shields clanged as the carts rolled over them, but the rocks were flung out and bounced off harmlessly over the protective cover of the shields. Thus the losses were very few and hardly anyone was so much as wounded, and instead of the expected slaughter there was much derision and loud laughter.

The Macedonians advanced toward the Danube and there Alexander was seized with a longing to visit the lands to the north of the river. But it was impossible to cross it without meeting a storm of arrows from the natives on the opposite bank. So Alexander commandeered all the fishing skiffs and dugout canoes that could be found, and collected them at a certain place. His men also stuffed tents and sheets of leather with hay or chaff and sewed them up tightly into balls which were light enough to float. In the dead of night, when neither moon nor stars looked down, the Macedonians paddled across the river using their homemade rafts and dugouts.

On the far bank of the Danube the maize stood high, taller than the helmets of the Macedonian soldiers. Then all at once the corn shot up, tripling its former height. In the first light of dawn, the enemy were horrified to see a forest of spears bearing down on them. They quickly took to their heels and did not stay to fight.

Alexander called to them to come back. He offered them his friendship on condition that they supply soldiers from their ranks to go with him on the campaign he was planning. "We are marching to the end of the world," he told them, to test their courage.

Then they crowded around him in large numbers, eager to join his army.

Alexander also marched west to win over various tribes to be his allies. His name flew like the wind from mouth to mouth and from land to land. Ambassadors from distant countries arrived at his camp. They all told him they were not his enemies and they would march with him if he wished. He enlisted many of them into his ranks.

Even Celtic warriors came on horseback from the upper Danube, tall men who thought well of themselves. Alexander appreciated their plain speaking and he offered hospitality to these strangers who had traveled so far to see him.

As they drank together and grew merry, he asked them what they feared most. "We are afraid of nothing," said the Celts, "except that the sky may fall, because it is so high."

This answer pleased Alexander and he asked them next, "And what do you value most?"

"Your friendship," replied the Celts.

Then Alexander told them that they were indeed his friends and he gave them generous presents. And they rode back to the upper Danube and spread Alexander's fame throughout their territory.

5

Alexander Punishes Thebes

AMONG the Greeks, there were many who had forgotten how magnanimously the King of Macedonia had treated them after the battle of Chaeronea. Now that Philip was dead and Alexander far away with his army, powerful orators in Athens and Thebes began rousing the people against the Macedonians. One wounded soldier in particular was paraded everywhere. "I fought by the Danube in the Macedonian army," he said, "and it was there that I got these wounds. I saw Alexander killed in battle. It happened before my very eyes."

Then the Thebans rose in rebellion and murdered two captains of the Macedonian guard whom King Philip had left behind in the citadel of Thebes.

As soon as Alexander learned of this, he struck camp and set off for Thebes, using forced marches. So rapidly did he cross the intervening mountains, rivers and plains that no one believed the patrols who brought the news that Alexander and his army were approaching. "They must be Greek soldiers returning home from Asia," said the orators. "Alexander is dead."

Then fresh scouts arrived. "It is Alexander who is at hand," they confirmed. "Tomorrow he will be at the city's gates."

"And which Alexander is it, pray?" jeered the orators. "Are we to tremble if some upstart Alexander or other has made himself King of Macedonia?"

The next morning, when the man they believed dead

stood outside the walls of Thebes, their consternation was great.

Alexander wished to spare the Thebans as his father had done before him. All he demanded was that they should hand over to him the men who had instigated the rebellion with their treacherous speeches, and also the murderers of the two captains.

The Thebans refused. They sallied forth at night and killed the Macedonian sentries.

At this, Alexander gave the signal to attack. The Macedonian guard within the city's fortress fell upon the Thebans in the rear and they were utterly defeated. Many houses were burned down and riderless horses galloped through the streets that were littered with the bodies of the slain.

Alexander had the city of Thebes razed to the ground, sparing only the house in which the poet Pindar was born, and those of the friends of the Macedonians. Thirty thousand Thebans were sold into slavery.

Later Alexander regretted his ruthlessness. When, for instance, he heard that Athens had given sanctuary within its walls to fugitives from Thebes, he did not insist on their being handed over to him.

6

Alexander Visits Diogenes and the Oracle at Delphi

AFTER this victory, the other Greek city-states sent ambassadors to Alexander, who was now in Corinth. There it was decided for the second time to launch an expedition against the Persians, and all the states except Sparta promised to supply cavalry, lancers and archers. Alexander was chosen to lead the expedition and appointed Captain of the League, as his father, Philip, had been after the battle of Chaeronea.

Famous artists and men of learning from all of Greece came to Corinth to pay their respects to Alexander. In those days, the philosopher who had the reputation of being the wisest man in Greece, second only to Aristotle, was one named Diogenes. To show his contempt for all display of worldly wealth, he chose to sleep in a barrel. It so happened that Diogenes too was in Corinth at that time, and Alexander expected that he would come and see him as the other philosophers had done, for the King would have liked very much to hear the wise man's views on the intended march to Asia. But Diogenes did not come.

So Alexander went to see him in the cypress grove where he lived. Diogenes was sitting on the bare earth when Alexander approached him, and the monarch asked the scholar if there was anything he could do to please him. Diogenes glanced up quickly at the young King, whose shadow fell across him. "You can step to one side," was his only request. "You are keeping the sun off me."

Then Alexander turned to the Companions, who were making fun of the sage. "If I were not Alexander, then I would like to be Diogenes," he told them.

The grand expedition that Alexander was planning was so important to him that he also wanted to consult the oracle of the god Apollo at Delphi. At certain times the god would answer questions from suppliants through the mouth of a prophetess; that is, whenever smoke emerged from a crack in the ground over which the temple was built.

When Alexander arrived in Delphi, however, it was not

14

the hour when the oracle consented to speak, and the priestess refused to allow him to enter the temple. But so strong was Alexander's wish to embark on his campaign that he forced his way into the temple and demanded an oracle there and then. Whereupon the priestess exclaimed, "Who can resist you, my son!"

"What further oracle do I need?" cried Alexander. "Have I not received the prophecy I wanted from the lips of the priestess? If I am indeed irresistible, I shall return from Asia victorious!"

7

Alexander Refuses the Ambassadors of Darius

DARIUS, Great King of Asia, called himself the King of Kings. All the countries that bordered on his domain owed him allegiance and paid him tribute. No other sovereign ruled over such a mighty empire. Persia, Media, Babylon and Egypt were all his vassals.

He sent his ambassadors to Pella too, to demand tribute from Alexander, just as his predecessor, Ochos, had sent envoys to King Philip.

Alexander received the Persians at a gathering of his friends, and he entertained them ceremoniously. They laughed and feasted and had no doubt that their mission would be a success until Alexander started to tell them a story.

"You must know," he began, "that my father Philip

had a nest concealed beneath his throne. On this nest a hen sat brooding, a bird that was half black and half white. During all the years of King Philip's reign, that black and white hen laid him a golden egg every day in the nest beneath the throne. So when the ambassadors of the Great King of Asia came from Susa to pay him a visit, it was no hardship for Philip to present them with boxes of golden eggs. But when my father died, the black and white hen went into deep mourning for him. Her grief was so great that she has quite forgotten how to lay, and that is how the matter stands even to this very day. And so, you envoys of King Darius, that is why I have nothing to give you this time, for there is not a single golden egg in any of the boxes."

Alexander had his men bring in three boxes, and when the lids were thrown back, the boxes were completely empty.

"And that, I fear, is how it will remain forevermore, for the black and white hen is inconsolable in her sorrow," concluded Alexander.

At this the envoys of King Darius started to their feet. Their faces were flushed with wrath, and their lips tightly pursed, holding back the angry words they did not speak. But their expressions said enough.

Alexander kept his cheerful composure and as the ambassadors mounted their horses, he bade them to be sure to tell the Great King that Macedonians and Greeks alike were eagerly looking forward to the day when they could repay the visit, and it would not be long before they came.

8

Alexander Sets Off on His Great Expedition

Now the time had arrived, and outside Pella a large army was mustered for the great expedition. There were ten thousand Macedonians, who fought with spear and sword; two thousand Macedonian cavalry and another two thousand Greek horsemen; ten thousand mercenaries who made up the infantry; five thousand archers; and sundry fighting men from many other nations. In all, some thirty-five thousand men and five thousand horses were gathered in readiness to march against the King of the Persians, who commanded a fighting force many times as great.

Before they set off on the great adventure, Alexander made each of his friends a present. To one he gave an estate, to another a village from the Crown Lands, to the third a studfarm, to the fourth the dues from a certain port.

"And what have you left for yourself?" asked Perdiccas, who was one of his generals.

"The hope of victory," replied Alexander.

"That hope I will share with you. I want nothing else," said Perdiccas, and he returned his gift to Alexander.

Then they all clamored to give him back their presents.

It was spring when Alexander took leave of his mother, Olympias, and of the philosopher, Aristotle. The trees were laden with blossoms and a shining carpet of flowers stretched before the feet of the army as it set out.

After marching twenty days, Alexander reached the coast from which Asia can actually be seen. It was here that the Persian king Xerxes had built two bridges of ships, more than one hundred years before, to convey his vast army into Europe. His object was to destroy the temples of the Greeks and to set the city of Athens on fire. Twice these bridges had been broken up by the onslaught of the stormy seas, and Xerxes had had the waves beaten as a punishment.

Now it was Alexander who stood on the shores of the Hellespont ready to avenge the crimes of the Persians. The army, under the command of Parmenion, began the crossing where the straits are narrowest. There were one hundred and seventy large galleys as transports, and innumerable canoes for the baggage.

Alexander and the Companions paid a visit to the ruins of Troy, and the King himself steered their ship into the bay that is known to this day as the Bay of the Achaeans. He tossed a golden bowl into the sea as a sacrifice to Poseidon, and as soon as he was close enough to the land, he hurled a javelin. It struck deep into the alien earth, and Alexander leaped after it from the prow of his ship. On the spot where he first trod the soil of Asia, he had altars built. Then he went to Troy with his Companions to pay his respects to the memory of Homer's heroes. Alexander and his dearest friend, Hephaestion, draped garlands around the graves of Achilles and his friend Patroclus, and they held games there in their honor. Nor did Alexander forget the defeated King Priam and the noble Hector, whom Achilles had killed in a duel and dragged behind his chariot around the walls of Troy in the fury of his rage.

When Alexander left Troy, he gave orders that the city, which had lain in ruins for a thousand years, should be rebuilt once more.

Then he mounted Bucephalus and rode off to rejoin his army.

9

Alexander's Victory by the Granicus

THE satraps of the Persian king were waiting on the bank of the river Granicus, their soldiers and horsemen massed in battle array, ready to bar the way to the advancing Macedonians and Greeks. There were Greek mercenaries serving with the Great King too, under the command of a general named Memnon. He had offered the Persian satraps a piece of advice which they had taken in very bad part.

"We ought to retreat before Alexander, so that his army breaks up and disintegrates before it comes to a battle," he told them. "We must destroy everything in his path that could possibly be useful to him. His soldiers are panting for booty and we must see to it that they go away empty-handed. Asia, we know, is immense, and if we allow the invaders to penetrate deep enough into the country, their one thought will be to turn back and go home again, and they will lose their faith in Alexander. Then we can fall on them like a pack of wolves pouncing on a flock of mangy sheep. Let us sacrifice a small portion of Asia, burn down the houses and destroy the crops, and in this way the Great King will preserve his empire as a whole."

Thus did Memnon speak, but the satraps did not trust him. Their pride would not allow them to withdraw without fighting. So the Persian army remained where it was on the banks of the Granicus, a modest river that rises in Mount Ida and flows its short course to the sea that divides Europe from Asia. Alexander had pitched his camp on the opposite bank of the same river.

The army of the Macedonians also included an experienced general who did not think that it was wise to risk a battle. This was Parmenion. "The Persians have too many advantages," he declared. "They occupy the steep bank of the river, for one thing. For another, the Granicus has a swift current and it is very deep in many places. Our losses in the initial attack are bound to be very heavy."

"We have sailed the seas already," answered Alexander. "It would be to our shame if we paid such a small river the compliment of being afraid of it."

Parmenion produced other arguments, "It is the month of May now, and according to our old traditions we Macedonians never give battle in May."

"Very well then. We shall decree two Aprils this year," retorted Alexander. "Then we need postpone the battle no longer. We shall attack today."

By then, however, it was already afternoon, and the sun was past its zenith.

"The sun is declining," Parmenion warned him. "It shows us that it is too late for a battle today."

"The sun has moved to the west and has crossed over to our side. It will shoot its golden arrows into the faces of the enemy and dazzle them, not us."

Alexander ordered his lancers to ford the river and scramble up the bank opposite. The Persian cavalry were

drawn up holding their front line, wedged in between the
river's edge and their own infantry, so that when a forest of
spears loomed up before them, the horses tried to break away.

The Macedonian cavalry, on the contrary, could maneuver freely and they attacked in a pincer movement, while
Alexander, with the Companions, thrust straight ahead and
made for the satraps. There was hand-to-hand fighting between the commanding officers of the two sides. The white
plume of Alexander's helmet flashed in the thick of the
melee. One javelin struck his cuirass at the joint, but it
bounced off again. A second lance wounded him in the
shoulder. The satrap Mithridates fell by Alexander's hand.
Then the King's helmet was split by a saber blow from the
satrap Rhosakes, but Alexander ran him through with his
sword. A third satrap raised his arm to strike another blow
at Alexander. In the nick of time Cleitus, one of Alexander's
Companions, chopped off the satrap's sword arm and so saved
the King's life.

Then the Persians fled. The battle by the Granicus had
lasted only a few hours, and already the gate to the Persian
Empire had been thrust wide open. Parmenion, Cleitus, Craterus, Hephaestion and Philotas, as well as all the other generals, now clamored for Alexander to push on immediately
for Susa and Persepolis.

But Alexander turned to the south instead. He wanted
to bring under his dominion all the coastal towns and harbors,
and only then, when these were assured, would he advance
into the interior of Asia.

Most of these cities opened their gates to him of their
own accord. Their inhabitants were Greeks who had been
ruled by Persian governors, appointed by the Persian king.
Now they were glad to throw off the hated foreign yoke.

Miletus, however, had to be taken by storm, and Halicarnassus was another town that Alexander had to fight for. He calculated that it would be a long siege, for it had stout walls and strong towers. But a couple of Macedonians were able to bring about the swift surrender of the city.

These two soldiers had been sitting in their tent drinking wine. When they had drunk enough to stiffen their courage, they grabbed their weapons and planted themselves before one of the gates of Halicarnassus. There they began provoking the defenders with torrents of abuse until five soldiers came outside to chase them away. But the two men were spoiling for a fight and refused to budge. Other Macedonians came to their aid, and when something like one hundred of the guards of Halicarnassus had sallied forth to join in the quarrel, the Macedonians took advantage of the confusion to enter the city and conquer it.

10

Alexander Unties the Gordian Knot

AMONG the cities that Alexander captured was the town of Gordium, named after Gordias, the King who had built it in ancient times. The King had a son whose name was Midas, and the gods fulfilled his every wish. When he asked them to give him the power of turning to gold everything he touched, they granted him this too. Thereupon even the bread he took in his hand turned to gold, and Midas realized that his wish had been too presumptuous.

One day, the god Apollo punished him, because Midas had proved himself a poor judge at a music competition. The god turned the King's ears into those of an ass. Midas concealed them under a tall helmet, and only the barber who cut his hair knew about his secret. The King forbade him to betray it to anyone, under pain of dire punishment. But the man could not keep it to himself, so he dug a hole in the ground and whispered the secret into it. "The King has asses' ears!" he breathed, and then he filled in the hole. Presently reeds began to grow where the hole had been, and they too started whispering in the wind, "The King has asses' ears!" And so the secret became known.

The gods had given Midas a chariot, whose shaft was secured with a rope made from the fibers of the cornel tree. The knot which held it was tied so cunningly that no one could find the ends, and according to an ancient belief the man who could undo this knot would reign over Asia.

Alexander tried to work it loose with his fingers and he struggled with it for a long time, but all in vain. He could tell by the faces of his Companions that they were deeply concerned that he had entered into such a dubious venture. At last he drew his sword and sliced through the knot. The ends of the cords came to light immediately and they pointed toward Alexander.

All who witnessed the event believed that the oracle had been fulfilled. When, in addition, a cloud appeared in a blue sky and a streak of lightning flashed from it, everyone present took it as an omen of divine affirmation.

11

Alexander Falls Dangerously Ill

ALEXANDER advanced into Cilicia over the Taurus Mountains. The rivers that flow through this land stay as cool and
clear for the whole of their course as they are when they rise
from their source. The most beautiful of these rivers is the
Cydnus. Its waters shimmer as brightly as if the river bed
were covered with sheets of white linen. The Cydnus flows
its entire length from the hills to the sea over a bed of stones
and it has no tributary mountain torrent to sully its purity
with mud.

Hot from hard riding, Alexander dived into the river.
He plunged into the icy water and it took his breath away.
The blood drained from his face; his arms and legs were
paralyzed. The King would have drowned immediately had
not a few brave souls come to the rescue and pulled him out
of the river. As they carried him into his tent only his eyes
betrayed his anguish, for he could not speak. Inside the tent
he collapsed, unconscious. Hours passed before he opened his
eyes again and it was only on the following day that his
speech returned. His doctor, Philip, ordered him another com-
plete day's rest. Then, he said, he would cure him by means
of a healing potion.

"This draught will have a very powerful effect," the
physician warned him. "You will lose consciousness again
and lie there like a corpse." Alexander was prepared to undergo any treatment.

The next day, he received a letter from Parmenion. It

had been brought by a courier who had ridden posthaste. Parmenion warned Alexander against his doctor. According to Parmenion, Philip had been promised one thousand talents by Darius, if he would kill the King. The cup he would give him would contain poison, not medicine.

Alexander was holding this letter in his hand when Philip entered his tent. As the King took the cup, he handed the physician the letter to read. Philip turned white, but he looked the King straight in the eye. "Have no fear," he said. "This drink will cure you. Why should I turn traitor and conspire to end a life I have watched over for so long? Parmenion is blind in his zeal. The Persian king has poisoned his mind."

Alexander reassured his doctor. "I have never doubted your loyalty," he said.

Everything came about as Philip had foretold. Once more the King was prostrated with fits of shivering and cramp, but after three days, he was able to get up from his couch. And when he stepped outside his tent with his physician by his side, the army acclaimed him, and the man who had saved his life, with tumultuous rejoicing.

Then Alexander gave orders to strike camp and to march against the Great King of Asia, who was advancing toward them with a powerful army.

In the south of Cilicia, there are three mountain passes leading to the frontier. This pleasant countryside could easily have been turned into a deathtrap if the Persians had sealed off these three passes. Yet Alexander found the mountain ridges unguarded.

In these mountains, Alexander paid a visit to a certain cave where a monster named Typhon had dwelt in the days when gods and Titans were still wrestling for the mastery of the earth. Typhon had succeeded in overpowering Zeus himself, the mightiest of the gods, and had dragged him into his lair. There he had drawn the sinews from the god's hands and feet, and had hung them upon the wall of the cave before the eyes of his prisoner. "I can keep you bound without fetters," he taunted Zeus. Confidently, Typhon left the cave to wreak new mischief elsewhere. But when he had gone, Hermes, the cunning god of merchants and thieves, and Pan, the god of mountains and meadows, slipped into the cave and restored the sinews to Zeus's limbs. So he was stronger than ever before, and when Typhon returned Zeus floored him with a throw and flung him into an abyss where his bones were shattered.

Alexander made a sacrifice to Zeus inside this cave, so that the god would bring victory to the army of the Greeks in their fight with the Asian colossus. Then the army marched through the pass that has borne the name of the Lion Gate since days of old.

12

Alexander Wins the Battle of Issus

THE enemy armies marched past one another in opposite directions through neighboring mountain valleys. The Macedonians were advancing inland, but Darius' host was heading for the seashore. And when they joined battle on the following day, the Persians were arrayed with their eyes toward their own country, while the Macedonians faced Macedonia.

True, Alexander had had his retreat cut off, but the Persian army was penned in on a narrow coastal strip between the mountains and the sea. It was on that bleak strand, with its reeds, heather and marsh, that the Battle of Issus took place.

As the armies attacked, shouting their terrifying battle cries and clashing their weapons, the echo reverberated from the mountains nearby and the walls of rock added their clamor to the din.

Alexander's cavalry and spearmen fell upon the encircling enemy, and with their first onslaught they pierced deep into the ranks of the Persians.

Darius took fright the moment he caught sight of Alexander. It was the Great King's brother and his generals who put up a fight and barred the way. They blocked the path of the Macedonians, and Alexander was wounded in the right hip.

The horses drawing the Persian king's war chariot were struck by the throwing spears of the Macedonians and, being wounded, they tried to bolt. Darius was flung from his chariot. He cast aside his royal cloak, tore off the blue and white turban he wore around his head and escaped from the confusion on a cavalry horse.

Swift as the wind the news spread through the Persian army that Darius had fled. The remaining soldiers thought of nothing but trying to save their own skins. Alexander pursued the fleeing host with one thousand horsemen and it was only when night fell that he turned back.

The imperial tent of King Darius with all its precious valuables was awaiting Alexander when he returned. He inspected the treasure and said, "Now we shall wash off the sweat of battle in Darius' bath."

"In Alexander's bath," his friend Hephaestion corrected him. "All this is yours now. Its owner has fled."

The most valuable of the spoils that the fugitive emperor had left behind for Alexander was the royal family—the Queen Mother, Sisygambis, his queen, Statira, two of their daughters and their son. The women were terrified that they would be shamefully treated by the conqueror, for such was the custom of war. But Alexander placed the tent with the royal prisoners under his personal protection. They were allowed to retain their own households, and everything that belonged to them.

The night was filled with jubilation as Greeks and Macedonians celebrated their victory. All at once there arose from the Queen's tent such shrill wails of lamentation that Alexander was startled. Then he was told that the women believed that Darius had been slain. His royal robes and his turban had been found on the battlefield, stained with blood. Alexander had a message sent to reassure the women. They had no need to worry about the King, for he had escaped.

The following day, Alexander took his friend Hephaestion with him to visit the Persian women. Darius' mother threw herself at Hephaestion's feet, for she thought that he must be Alexander. As Hephaestion stepped back, Sisygambis, realizing her error, looked up at Alexander, afraid. But pointing to Hephaestion, Alexander merely said, "You made no mistake, Mother. He too is Alexander."

Then Sisygambis spoke. "You are a king," she said, "and it is our duty to pray that the gods will bestow their favors on you, as we prayed formerly for King Darius. You have exceeded him in mercy and also in your good fortune. But you will find that we, who were once so exalted, are ready to bear with dignity the hard fate that has befallen us now."

Then Alexander comforted her and gave presents to the royal women. He took the little son of Darius in his arms, and the child was not afraid of the stranger, although he had never seen him before and could not understand the words he spoke. Touched by the boy's fearlessness, Alexander turned to Hephaestion saying, "I wish his father, too, had not run away from me." He promised the women that no Greek or Macedonian would enter their tent in the future.

On the battlefield, Alexander had three altars built. Then he set off with his army toward Syria.

13

Alexander Sends Parmenion to Damascus

PARMENION was sent on ahead to Damascus. His orders were to try to get possession of the treasure which Darius had dispatched there for safekeeping before the battle.

On the way the Macedonians met a man bearing a letter for Alexander from the governor of the city of Damascus. In this he begged the King to send him a troop of cavalry as quickly as possible, and he offered to hand over the imperial treasure to them.

Parmenion explained to the messenger that he had before him the very troop of horse requested in the letter, and he told the man to return to Damascus instead of going on to Alexander. The messenger, however, tried to reach Alexander by another route. In doing this, he delayed his return to Damascus, and the governor grew anxious, uncertain what to do. On no account did he want to hold the treasure in his city any longer, nor did he want to keep the noblemen whom Darius had also entrusted to his care. He persuaded these lords that he was having them escorted by a safe route into the interior of Asia where they and the treasure would be secure. Actually, however, he intended to betray them to Alexander.

Beneath the black wintry sky, men, horses, camels and mules set off. On the second day a snowstorm broke. The track vanished beneath a blanket of white, and trees and shrubs loomed up like ghosts through the driving snow. The biting cold pierced the thin clothes of the Persians. The situation was so desperate that nobles as well as porters broke into the treasure chests, in which were packed the heavy ceremonial robes and precious rugs, and they wrapped themselves for warmth in the royal purple. Through the bleak wilderness the caravan plodded on, arrayed in all its sumptuous magnificence.

Parmenion and his horsemen chanced to cross their path. The splendor of their garments misled the Macedonians, who thought that these were armed troops before them, and Parmenion gave orders to attack.

The Persians took flight, tearing off their precious trappings as they ran. In panic they seized the mules and camels, and the packs the animals were carrying fell to the ground.

And so, in the end, fabulous treasures lay scattered over the icy landscape. Tattered draperies hung from the bushes. Jewelry, golden vessels and harnesses, ceremonial weapons and the money to pay the wages of the mighty Persian army, as well as purple pavilions and robes encrusted with golden embroidery, all were trampled into the snow and the mud.

Parmenion's men did not have enough hands among them to pick up everything that was strewn on the ground. The sum of gold coin alone amounted to more than two thousand six hundred talents. The value of the wrought gold and silver was beyond measure.

Of the nobles who had accompanied the caravan, only a few escaped to join Darius.

14

Alexander Replies to a Letter from Darius

AFTER his flight from the battlefield the Persian emperor had taken refuge beyond the Euphrates. Quickly he gathered his cavalry about him. He knew Asia to be a vast continent, and so in spite of all his misfortunes, he still cherished the hope that he could defeat Alexander in another battle. True, he had lost an army, and he knew that those who were most dear to him were in the hands of the enemy. But only a small fraction of the entire Persian fighting force had been subdued by the Macedonians so far. Darius considered that he was still the Great King, for he remained the ruler of immeasurable lands.

He sent messengers to Alexander, and they took with them as presents a bridle, a ball, a chest filled with gold, and a sack of poppy seeds, together with a letter. This is what it said:

Darius, the friend of the gods, informs you, Alexander, that you must now hand back to me all you have stolen, my lands, cities, treasure and weapons, as well as my mother, my queen and my children. Then you must go home to your mother. I have sent you a bridle, so that you may learn to curb yourself; a ball for you to play with, for you are but a boy and not yet old enough to be a king; a chest of gold, so that you and your soldiers may not suffer want on the way home; and a sack of poppy seeds, so that you may count them for yourself, and learn how numerous are the soldiers I have at my command.

Alexander took this letter and the gifts of Darius and he held them up so all the army could see them. He read the letter aloud to the assembled Macedonians and Greeks, and they roared so loudly with laughter that Darius' envoys shrank in fear. Alexander gave them a letter in reply to that of the Persian king, which read:

I have come to Asia to avenge the crimes committed by the Persians against the Greeks, and to punish you, Darius, for the many murders you have instigated. That you are a friend of the gods I cannot believe, for they have given the victory to me and not to you. Therefore, when you write to me in the future, address me as the King of Asia, and your overlord. If you come to me in all submission, I will allow your mother, your queen and your children to return to you. However, if you believe that next time the sun will rise on your good fortune and not on mine, then have the courage to meet me once more on the field of battle, and do not run away again.

With this letter, Alexander dismissed the ambassadors of King Darius and he gave them a peppercorn and a message. "Tell Darius, that I found the number of poppy seeds great indeed, but that when I crunched a few of them between my teeth, I found them soft and insipid. Let Darius do the same with this peppercorn I send him. And tell him this. The ball he gave me is a sign that the whole round earth will fall into my hands. The bridle is a symbol to me that I shall harness the nations that are now ruled by Darius. And the gold in the chest is a token of the tribute he will pay me as long as he lives."

Then the Persian messengers mounted their horses in great haste and galloped away toward the Euphrates.

15

Alexander Creates a King

ALEXANDER now marched on toward Phoenicia. Envoys from many Phoenician cities came to meet him and they offered the King golden wreaths as a sign of their voluntary submission. Even the great city of Byblus did so, and King Strato handed over the city of Sidon to Alexander. Now Strato did not do this of his own accord but because the city's inhabitants forced his hand. When Alexander learned the truth, he deposed Strato and gave Hephaestion the task of finding the worthiest citizen and making him king instead.

Highly respected elders of the town led Hephaestion to a man whose name was Abdalon. Although he could trace his ancestry back to one of the royal founders of the city,

33

Abdalon worked as a gardener for a rich man. In spite of his hard lot, he was contented, and when Hephaestion and his companions entered the garden, Abdalon was busy weeding the flower beds. Hephaestion saluted the gardener as king. The party had brought with them the royal robes, and one of the men said, "Take this mantle and give us your gardener's smock. Alexander has appointed you to rule this city, which your forefathers governed so long ago."

Abdalon gazed up in bewilderment at Haphaestion and the men whom he knew. Was he dreaming, or were they playing a practical joke on him? But the attendants washed the soil from his hands and feet and decked him in the royal purple. Then they led him through the cheering crowds to the king's palace.

The wealthy people in the city were displeased with this choice, and as soon as Alexander heard of their opposition he sent for Abdalon to come to see him. When he entered, Alexander was surprised at the new King's regal bearing. "How was it possible for a man like you to live so patiently in such dire poverty?"

"As I had but few possessions, I had few worries," was the reply.

"You will make a good king," said Alexander.

16

Alexander Conquers Tyre and Gaza

THE mightiest of all the Phoenician cities was Tyre. It was a queen of Tyre who had founded Carthage long before, and every year Carthaginians came to the mother city to celebrate the great event.

Tyre itself consisted of two towns: an Old City, situated on the mainland, and the New City, which had been built on an island. New Tyre had never been taken by storm. King Nebuchadnezzar had laid siege to the island city for thirteen years, but he had never conquered it.

When Alexander demanded that he should be allowed to enter New Tyre in order to sacrifice to Herakles in the temple there, the citizens refused to admit him. "There is a temple to Herakles in Old Tyre as well," they declared.

This answer incensed Alexander and he vowed he would enter Tyre even if it kept its gates locked. "Herakles came to me in a dream," he said. "With his own hands, he handed me the city's title deeds over the wall and led me inside."

The Tyrians heard this with alarm. And when the god Apollo appeared to one of the city fathers also in a dream, and told him that he was going over to Alexander's side, so great was the consternation that the priests put chains around the statue of Apollo and nailed it fast to its pedestal. Yet, in spite of all the evil omens, the Tyrians were determined to resist. They put their trust in the straits between the town and the mainland, for these were very deep and a strong current flowed through them, especially when the south wind blew from Africa.

Alexander devised a plan for building a mole to link the mainland with the island. When the Tyrians learned of his intentions, they laughed at the very idea. Where could he get enough stones to build such an immense construction which would have to rest on the sea bed?

Alexander found the stones he needed by having the Old City of Tyre completely demolished and dumped into the sea. He had the cedars of Lebanon felled and rocks hewn from quarries. He himself hoisted stones on his shoulders, as an encouragement to the men whose task it was to carry these loads.

For seven months the building went on, and time and again this road into the sea was shattered by storms or damaged by the ramming ships of the Tyrians. But at last a mighty causeway sixty paces wide stretched out toward the island, and wooden siege towers, as high as the city's walls, rose directly before the ramparts of Tyre. The desperate islanders had two ships filled with burning naptha, which they launched against these towers, and they sent them up in flames. The towers were built a second time.

Meanwhile about eighty Phoenician ships had transferred their allegiance to the Macedonian king, and the Greek fleet of ships arrived on the scene as well, to serve as reinforcements. Alexander could now attack Tyre from three sides at once. The Tyrians defended themselves feverishly, using every weapon they could—planks of wood with scythes attached to the end, burning shields, torches of pitch, and harpoons—but still the walls were breached.

Tyre fell, left in the lurch not only by its daughter city

of Carthage but by the other Phoenician cities as well. Not a stone was left standing in New Tyre either.

To conquer Gaza, the most powerful city in Syria, Alexander had ramps of earth and stones built up to the height of the walls, while underground passages were bored beneath the walls and into the heart of the town itself.

Alexander was standing on a ramp one day when a clod of earth fell on his helmet, dropped from a great height by a raven. The bird swooped down in the wake of the clod, as if to see what damage it had done, but it dropped so low that it became entangled in the ropes of one of the siege engines.

As the raven was considered a bird of omen, Alexander called for the soothsayer Aristander, in whom he had great faith, and he asked him to interpret the incident. This is how Aristander read the signs: Alexander would indeed capture the town, but during the engagement, he would fall into great peril. And so it came about. Alexander was wounded by an arrow that penetrated deep into his left shoulder. But a week later, Gaza, too, was conquered.

17

Alexander Shows Himself a Friend of the Jews

DURING this same period when Alexander was besieging Tyre and Gaza, he also wrote letters to all the cities in neighboring countries, asking them for their help. One of these

37

letters was sent to Jaddua, the High Priest in Jerusalem. The Jews were ordered to send to Alexander the tribute they had formerly sent to Darius, and also supplies of corn and meat, as the Macedonian army was short of food.

Jaddua took counsel with the other priests and then he wrote to Alexander as follows: "I have sworn an oath to the Persian king, to serve him loyally as long as he lives."

Having taken Tyre and Gaza, Alexander then advanced on Jerusalem, and the Jews who lived there trembled at the thought of his wrath and called on Almighty God to help them. As Jaddua prayed in the Temple, a voice spoke to him: "Open the gates of the city and go forth to meet Alexander, wearing upon your head the golden diadem with My name upon it." So Jaddua went out to meet Alexander on the hill which overlooks Jerusalem, and a great procession followed him.

When Alexander caught sight of the High Priest, his anger vanished. He dismounted and went forward on foot to greet him, and he made an obeisance before him. Alexander's Companions looked at one another indignantly, believing that their king must have been bewitched. "Have you forgotten that this man before whom you bow, is the one you were going to punish?" asked Parmenion, going up to him. "I have not bowed before him but before his God," said Alexander and turning to Jaddua, he told him, "I wish to live in peace with you and I am prepared to grant you a favor."

Then Jaddua spoke. "For us Jews," he said, "the seventh day is the Lord's Day. Grant us, therefore, that every seventh year shall be free of tribute, taxes or dues for us. Give us a charter with your seal upon it." And Alexander granted the Jews this exception, wherever they might live.

After this, the Jews too were eager to serve in Alexander's army and he had many of them enrolled. They included a man named Mosolam, whom they considered to be their finest archer. He could hit a cap thrown into the air from a distance of one hundred paces.

When Alexander led his army southward, there was much grumbling. He was making them conquer Egypt too, it seemed, instead of marching straight for Susa in the east, where the Lord of Asia and Egypt sat in his palace. Even the soothsayers said that the signs were more propitious for an attack on Susa rather than Egypt, for a raven kept flying toward them from the south, and as soon as it was over Alexander's head, it persistently swerved to the east. When this happened for the third time, Mosolam took aim and shot the bird, so that it fell dead at the King's feet.

The soothsayers were horrified and declared that the Jewish archer had committed a sacrilege.

Mosolam, however, calmly stooped and picked up the dead raven from the ground. "How can this bird possibly foretell the future of a king and his army?" he asked. "Why, it could not even foresee its own fate, or it would never have flown straight to the spot where it met my arrow!"

Then Alexander praised Mosolam both for his deed and his words, and from that time on, he kept him in his personal bodyguard. In better spirits, the army continued its march into Egypt.

18

Alexander Founds Alexandria

TEN years before Alexander, the Persian king Ochos had marched into Egypt. He had dealt so cruelly with the people that the Nile had been dyed red, and he had slaughtered the Holy Bull of Apis as a butcher kills an ox from the fields.

Alexander was greeted as a liberator. The cities opened their gates to him, and in a triumphal procession the Egyptians led him into Memphis, where the Nile stretches out its seven arms to embrace the sea. In the temple at Memphis Alexander received the crowns of both Upper and Lower Egypt and the titles due to the Pharaoh. He was now a Son of the Sun in the eyes of the Egyptians. Alexander made no distinction between Greeks and Egyptians, and he placed the gods of Egypt on a level with those of Greece, Ammon with Zeus and Horus with Apollo. At the sacrifice which he made to the Bull of Apis, Alexander remembered another bull. This was the one that had carried Europa, a king's daughter, across the sea from Asia to Crete, where she had borne three sons to Zeus, among them Minos, the wisest of all kings.

As a compliment to the Egyptians, and also to remind the Greeks and the Macedonians of their homeland, Alexander sent to Greece for the finest of their performers and athletes to entertain the troops. Games and contests were held in the shadow of the Pyramids, and they were conducted with as much ceremony as those at Olympia. In this way Alexander created bonds of friendship among the nations.

Accompanied by a division of archers and cavalry, the

King traveled down that branch of the Nile that extends farthest to the west. When he came to the sea, he observed that the coast there offered a site for a harbor which was unsurpassed in the entire Mediterranean Sea.

The small island of Pharos sheltered the land in bad weather against the onslaught of the waves, and a tongue of land screened the spacious bay from the open sea. There was also a lagoon that opened inland, which seemed ideal for a harbor basin. In addition, a strong undertow, flowing from west to east, carried away the mud from the Nile and thus would prevent the harbor bottom from silting up.

As Alexander looked out toward the little island, a verse from Homer's *Iliad* came into his mind: "Then an island rises from the storm-tossed seas at the mouth of Egypt's river, and Pharos is its name."

Alexander recited the words aloud, and he said to his Companions, "We could not wish for a better counselor than Homer."

The city was designed then and there. It was to include a port, a mole and a colossal lighthouse, to be situated on the island of Pharos. The ground plan was outlined with seeds of barley, laid on the black earth which the Nile carries down from the interior of Africa, and the shape of the city was that of a cape worn by a Macedonian warrior.

When the plan was finished and had been approved in all its detail, there was a great noise of rushing wings and a flock of birds flew in from the sea. They swooped on the barley laid out on the ground and not one single grain was left. Alexander was greatly perturbed when he saw this, and the Companions too were troubled. But Aristander, the soothsayer, held it to be a good omen. The city would furnish food for a multitude of people, he prophesied.

Then Alexander had the work started forthwith, and he gave the town his name.

19

Alexander Visits the Oasis of Siwah

MUCH farther to the west, deep in the desert, lies the oasis of Siwah, where the god Ammon had his oracle. Alexander was seized by a desire to consult it, although no pharaoh before him had ever visited the god in the desert. But both Herakles and Perseus, Alexander's heroes and models, had ventured on that journey and had received favorable answers to their questions. Cambyses, the Asian invader who, like Ochos, had scourged Egypt, had sent an army into the desert to destroy the oracle. The god was roused to anger and had overwhelmed the blasphemous intruders with a great sandstorm, which had buried them completely.

In Alexander's day the oracle of the god in the desert had an even greater reputation than those of Delphi and Dodona. Anyone who approached it did so at the risk of his life.

With incredible courage, Alexander dared to conquer this desert with a small army. It did not treat him as an enemy, however. At first, when he left the coast and turned south, there was nothing before him but wilderness and bare rock. The fiery breath of the desert and whirling columns of sand greeted him and his troops, but before their water supplies were exhausted, heavy clouds spread across the skies and veiled the blazing sun. The rain came pouring down in torrents and conjured up grass and flowers from the sand. The desert laid a carpet of green at Alexander's feet.

Twelve days later the little expedition reached the oasis of Siwah, with its abundant date palms and olive groves, its many springs and pools. Priests came out of the temple to meet the King and to tell him that he alone might enter the Holy of Holies, where the god Ammon stood in a golden barque.

The High Priest hailed Alexander as the Son of Ammon. Then the King put his questions to the god.

When he emerged from the temple once more, and his friends pressed him to tell them what answers he had received, he would say nothing. But the glory on his face revealed that he was well content. All who had accompanied Alexander to the oasis had seen for themselves the wonderful omens, and had heard the High Priest greet the King as the son of the god.

20

Alexander Discovers the Source of the Nile

ALEXANDER left the oasis of Siwah and crossed the great desert with his Companions until he returned to the city of Memphis that stands on the Nile. This journey took him eighteen days. Here, in the ancient capital of the Egyptian kings, envoys were waiting to greet the new Pharaoh—ambassadors from the Greek city-states, from Pella and from many other lands.

Alexander wished to consult the Egyptian priests, who were men of great learning and who could explain many things that were a puzzle even to his tutor Aristotle. When Alexander asked these wise men to tell him where the Nile rose, and how it happened that every year it flooded the land and made the soil fertile even to the edge of the desert, there was a long pause before they replied. Then they said, "Whoever wishes to learn such a great secret must keep a nightlong vigil within the temple, so that his spirit may be receptive."

Alexander spent that night in the temple. And so great was his longing to learn the source of the Nile that his spirit spread its wings and hovered over him like a bird. The body of the King lay before the altar as if he were dead, but the bird that was his spirit skimmed through the air, following the course of the Nile. Although it was night, it could see the glistening waters, and it flew the entire length of Egypt. It crossed Nubia and came to a land where the river comes tumbling down from a great height, as if cascading down a mighty staircase. Then the bird saw that the Nile stretches out two arms to its sources. One arm, which is white, reaches into a gleaming lake which is white too, because the snow of mountain peaks is mirrored in its surface. The other arm is blue and it ends in a lake that takes its color from the sky. These lakes lie in the country of the Ethiopians, close to the Equator. And then a great rain fell and this caused the waters of the Nile to rise. When the deluge stopped, the level of the river dropped once more.

In this way Alexander's spirit solved the great mystery. It flew back down the Nile to Memphis and roused the rigid

44

body that lay in the temple. When the priests arrived the next morning, they were astounded to hear Alexander tell them the very things he had wished to know.

They were even more astonished when he sent men with boats to sail up the Nile as far as the Equator, in order to confirm everything his spirit had seen on its flight through the air.

Now that he had won the kingdom of the Pharaohs, Alexander was as eager to march eastward as his men. There he would occupy the thrones of Babylon and Persepolis, so that Asia and Africa would be united with the countries of the west, and he himself would be Lord of the Earth.

21

Alexander Pays His Respects to a Dead Queen

IT was about this time that Darius wrote a second letter to Alexander. Now he addressed him as a king and a brother. He asked for the release of his mother, his queen and his children, against a ransom of ten thousand talents. Of even greater significance was the fact that he also offered Alexander half his empire and the hand of one of his daughters in marriage. Alexander would reign from Greece to the Euphrates, and Darius from the Euphrates to India. "Let us live side by side in friendship and keep the peace," Darius proposed, "each the ruler of one half of the world."

Alexander had just arrived in Tyre when he received this letter. He summoned his counselors and his closest friends, and he placed the letter before them. His expression betrayed nothing of what he himself thought of the offer, but he saw at once that all his closest friends except Hephaestion took no trouble to conceal their joy. Why should they march on and undergo fresh dangers, when they had the chance to return to Greece and Macedonia covered with glory? Wasn't half the world enough?

Alexander turned to the oldest of his generals, Parmenion, and he asked him for his advice. "If I were Alexander, I should accept Darius' proposals," he exclaimed.

"So should I, if I were Parmenion," was Alexander's reply.

Parmenion defended his point of view. "I served your father long enough to know that King Philip would not have spoken otherwise."

"I am not King Philip," retorted Alexander.

To Darius he wrote that if he came to meet him as a vassal, he would hand over to him his mother, wife and children. If not, he must be prepared for an encounter on the field of battle. And Alexander ordered his army to be ready to set off the next day.

That same night, however, he canceled this order. One of the Queen's household, a Persian named Tireus, brought him news that Statira, the consort of Darius, had died.

Alexander was greatly dismayed. He turned to Tireus and said, "The Queen must be given a burial as befits her rank and her dignity."

All of Alexander's army paid their last respects to the dead queen. Only when this had been done did the King give the signal for his men to continue the march eastward.

It was the same Tireus who broke the bitter news to the Persian king too. Darius struck his forehead and began to lament aloud, "Woe is me! What evil fortune pursues the Persians, that their queen must die a prisoner and forfeit the right to a royal funeral."

"The King of the Macedonians has held up his advance, so that the dead queen could be given a worthy burial," answered Tireus. "His whole army has bowed before her. My mistress had to forgo only one thing during her imprisonment, and that was the light of your countenance—may the gods restore it soon to its full glory. Alexander has guarded the honor of the royal household as jealously as if they were the women of his own family. He is as noble in victory as he is terrible in war."

Now Darius rose up in all his grief, but he was determined to risk one last battle against Alexander. In great haste he had his army reinforced and new weapons forged. A muster was called from all the lands of Asia, and the levies were commanded to assemble by the banks of the swift-flowing Tigris to thrust back the army of Macedonians and Greeks.

22

Alexander Crosses the Euphrates and Strays into Great Danger

ALEXANDER marched on to the Euphrates and he ordered a bridge to be built across the river. It was a bridge of ships, with tree trunks laid from vessel to vessel and secured with chains. The army built this bridge so energetically that it was completed in four days. The night before the crossing Alexander rode around his camp to see if the soldiers and horsemen had everything they needed. Hephaestion reproached the King. "You should be sleeping now like all the rest, for you bear a greater burden than anyone else."

"If any of my soldiers suffer want, then I am the most concerned," replied Alexander.

In the first light of dawn, hoofbeats thundered over ships and tree trunks. It was a miracle that so few horses fell into the river and that the bridge held. "It will still be there when we return," marveled Cleitus, the general who had saved the King's life in the first battle.

"You are mistaken," said Alexander. "It will be destroyed this very day."

They were all surprised at his words and Philotas, the son of Parmenion, asked, "But who is there to do it? There is no sign of the enemy for miles."

"We shall destroy it ourselves," said Alexander. "We shall burn every ship and every tree trunk."

"But doesn't that mean cutting off the way back to Macedonia?" asked Parmenion.

"Darius will realize that too," said Alexander, "and for him it will be a sign that we are confident he will never defeat us. It will shake him to the core."

The bridge that had been built with such ingenuity and zeal was broken up and destroyed. Alexander was the first to throw a lighted torch into one of the ships. Blazing from stem to stern, they floated downstream toward the city of Babylon.

But Alexander marched on with his army in the direction of the Tigris. Beyond the river the daylight grew dark, as if the land were smothered in fog. But it was clouds of smoke that came rolling toward them.

"All we have burned is one bridge," said Alexander, "but Darius has ordered his people to set fire to the whole countryside. That is a sure sign he is afraid."

The Macedonians attempted the crossing of the Tigris at several fords, but even these places were dangerous, for the river bed was littered with pebbles carried down by the many tributary mountain torrents and swept along by the current. The water reached up to the horses' necks, and many of the soldiers were washed away, together with their packs. Then the army grew more agitated than before a battle, for they thought of nothing but the danger of losing the spoils they had captured so far.

Alexander turned to address his men. "Whatever is lost will be replaced, I promise you. After the next battle, the gates of Babylon, Susa and Persepolis will open before you, and there you may help yourselves for every man of you will find more booty than he can carry. Therefore all you have to do is to see that you and your weapons reach the opposite bank of the river."

Ropes were stretched from bank to bank for the soldiers to hold onto, and so, half wading, half swimming, they made their way through the water. That is how Alexander got all his army safely across the Tigris.

The Persian cavalry came galloping toward them over the scorched earth, but it was too late. They were either routed or killed in battle, or else taken prisoner. In one of these skirmishes a soldier clad in a Greek helmet, armor and shield attacked Alexander from behind. Two Macedonians standing near suddenly saw to their horror that a Greek sword was raised against the person of their king. They both flung their spears and the man sank to the ground, pierced through.

"Traitor!" cried Alexander, beside himself with rage. "What have I done to you that you would attack me from behind? Were you hoping for the reward that Darius, fearing for his own life, has offered for my murder? Treacherous Greek!"

Then the man answered in Persian and it was revealed that he was not a Greek at all, but a Persian who had dared to enter Alexander's army as a partisan, a member of the resistance. "My king has promised me nothing, for he does not know of my existence. It was my own idea to kill you because you deserve to die. You have taken away our country's freedom and the crown from our king. But Darius with his army will accomplish what I have failed to do."

With this threat on his lips, he died. Alexander was impressed by such courage and he had the soldier buried like a hero from his own army.

23

Alexander Plays a Trick on Darius

DARIUS had assembled his army beyond the Tigris at the village of Gaugamela. This name means "The House of the Camel." Vast hordes from many parts of Asia had been gathered together to form that mighty host. The Persian king had more than one thousand chariots whose wheels were fitted with scythes, and their purpose was to mow down the ranks of the enemy.

The Greeks and Macedonians were alarmed when they saw the armed camp of Darius. Therefore Alexander had a fortified camp pitched at a safe distance, for he did not wish to attack until the following day.

On the eve of the great battle a Macedonian herald appeared in the camp of the Persians and announced that Alexander had sent him to speak with the Great King. So he was led into the presence of Darius. But first he had to pass the numerous Persian units and their campfires, and although he saw the whole strength of that enormous fighting force, his face betrayed no trace of fear.

Darius received the envoy courteously. He still nursed a secret hope that Alexander would call off the battle at the last moment and then agree to the partition of the empire. A table was laid to entertain the Macedonian. And just as earlier they had deliberately guided him past warriors and all their arms, so now they displayed for his benefit all the wealth and luxury of the Great King's tent. And once again his expression revealed nothing.

Darius avoided speaking of the war, and the emissary too wasted no words about the forthcoming encounter. He allowed himself to be entertained and drank from the heavy golden goblet that stood before him. This cup was a work of art, and when he had emptied it the Macedonian placed it inside his cloak.

The Persians stared at the man, Darius most of all. "Has your king so few golden vessels of his own that you must take the cup from my table?" he asked indignantly.

"On the contrary," answered the Macedonian. "It is the custom at Alexander's court for each man to take away the cup he empties, to show his respect for the King."

Everyone sitting around that table was amazed at these words, and they all marveled at the candor with which the envoy spoke.

Then the satrap Pasarges approached the Great King and whispered a few words in his ear. A shadow flitted over Darius' face and he fixed his eyes on his uninvited guest.

"This is no herald," Pasarges cried aloud. "It is Alexander himself, disguised in a messenger's cloak!"

They all leaped to their feet, but the Macedonian, sword in one hand and golden cup in the other, had already cleared a path for himself to the door of the tent. The moment he was outside he swung himself onto the back of the King's horse which was standing by ready for Darius to mount. And as everyone stood there hypnotized at the sight of a Macedonian astride the charger of the Great King, the stranger galloped off through the camp and no one threw a javelin after him or shot an arrow. He had advantage enough and no other horse could overtake him.

The Persian king never found out for sure whether or not it was Alexander himself who had come into his presence with such audacity. But the news spread like wildfire through the Persian camp that the King of the Macedonians had carried off a golden goblet from his enemy's table and ridden away on one of his horses. And terror clutched their hearts.

24

Alexander Wins the Battle of Gaugamela

It was a night when plains and rivers shone, for the moon in the sky was full. Then, all at once, the silver orb became overcast. Heavy shadows fell across the land and the Tigris turned to black. Macedonians and Greeks came running out of their tents, and many of them took the sudden uncanny darkness for an omen of approaching evil. Alexander sent for his soothsayers and wise men.

"The darkness is the work of the three gods who guide the course of the sun, the moon and the earth," they declared. "They wish to announce their will to the Greeks before the battle. Since the sun belongs to us Greeks and the moon to the Asian peoples, it is a good sign that the moon is dimmed and not the sun. This eclipse of the moon means the defeat and destruction of the Persians."

Alexander had this interpretation of the seers made known throughout his army, for he knew that the word of a soothsayer carries more weight than that of a king.

From the camp of the Persians arose a great wave of noise that frightened the Macedonians. On hearing it, Parmenion implored Alexander to attack at once. "The darkness will be our ally," he said. "By day, the mighty army of the Asians will overwhelm us, like the sea."

"We are soldiers, not thieves in the night," replied Alexander. "It is beneath our dignity to steal a victory." And he added, "In any case, to attack by night is as hazardous as going into a cave without a light."

He sent all his company commanders to rest and then he too went into his tent to sleep.

The next morning the whole of the army was on its feet early and although everyone else had breakfasted, Alexander was still asleep. Parmenion had to call him by name three times before he awoke. "How can you sleep so soundly?" wondered Parmenion. "This day will decide the fate of us all."

"The gods have decided it already," said Alexander.

In full view of all his soldiers, he armed himself for the battle. First he put on a light tunic of Sicilian workmanship, and over this he buckled on a corselet made of two thicknesses of stout linen, which had fallen to him as booty after the Battle of Issus. His helmet was fashioned of burnished iron and so skillfully toughened and hammered that it gleamed like polished silver. His sword, the work of a Cretan master craftsman, was light in his hand.

Alexander surveyed the battlefield. Darius had had every tree and bush cleared away so that nothing would hinder the movement of his many soldiers. "He has cleared the field for us too," observed Alexander.

Spies had reported to him that the Persian king had had the earth strewn with iron spikes, as a trap for the Macedonian cavalry. "We shall drive his horsemen toward those places," said Alexander. He arranged that the ranks break formation when the scythed chariots attacked, so that the teams of horses would go racing through along empty lanes. "Thus they will be no use to Darius and do us no harm either," said the King. Then he addressed his men.

"We have defeated this King of Kings once before, and on that occasion he ran away from us. He is so afraid of us that he has laid waste broad stretches of his own kingdom.

For the last three days his army has been pinned down here, and they are already exhausted by the weight of their own armor. On this battlefield the gods will grant us the victory, and put all of Asia into our hands."

Then the army of the Greeks and the Macedonians shouted "Alexander! Alexander!" again and again. And the edges of the nearby mountains quivered in the rays of the rising sun. By Alexander's side stood the seer Aristander, wearing a white mantle and with a golden fillet around his brow. His hand pointed to the sky where an eagle was circling, and as Alexander gave the signal to attack the eagle dropped like a stone and swooped down on the camp of Darius. Then not a man in that army, Greek or Macedonian, doubted any longer that victory would be theirs.

Alexander's army charged, and the scythed chariots hurtled toward them at full tilt. The ranks opened and the chariots raced along between the tall fences of bristling spears. The charioteers fell, an easy target for Macedonian arrows, and the chariots slewed over, out of control. Their scythes ripped long furrows in the ground of the battlefield.

Alexander ordered the left flank of his army to withdraw and the Persians immediately started pursuing them so wildly that they left a gap in their own front. Into this gap charged Alexander and his cavalry, and soon he was face to face with the Great King. Darius hurled his lance at Alexander and missed him. Then the Persian monarch lost his nerve for the second time. And although his personal bodyguard defended him gallantly, and as many Macedonians as Persians were killed in this action, Darius leaped down from his war chariot and galloped away on horseback. Seeing this, his soldiers fled too. Alexander was proclaimed Great King of Asia on the battlefield of Gaugamela. That night the fires of victory flared so high into the sky that the very stars were blotted out.

25

Alexander Marches to Babylon

NEXT Alexander turned south with his army to march on the city of Babylon. The Persian king Xerxes, who had desecrated the temples of Greece, had also destroyed the Marduk temple in Babylon. Alexander sent messengers ahead with orders to re-erect the statue of the god, and to restore the temple to all its former glory. As in Egypt, Alexander was greeted as a liberator wherever he went.

On their march the army passed a blazing spring of petroleum, and soon afterward they saw a bitumen lake which gazed up at the sky like a huge eye of black. The people living nearby carried away big barrels of oil and poured it along the edge of the highway. They set the oil on fire until the flames streaked across the flat ground like lightning flashes, making a ceremonial flare path to delight the Greeks and Macedonians as they marched along.

The satrap Mazaios came out to meet them from Babylon. He had fought bravely at Gaugamela—and longer than his king. Now, however, he wished to save the wonderful city he governed.

The streets of Babylon were strewn with flowers and the

houses were festooned with garlands. Clouds of incense rose from every altar. When he received Alexander, Mazaios presented him with a lion and a panther, each in a golden cage. Hundreds of horses and head of cattle were waiting for the army that had defeated Darius. Minstrels sang songs in praise of Alexander and astrologers performed solemn dances, symbolizing the course of the constellations and the changing of the seasons. So, to the acclamation of the Babylonians, Alexander occupied the royal palace and took possession of the incalculable riches it contained.

The Greeks and Macedonians could not get over their astonishment at the wonders of Babylon. The city's walls were so wide that there was room for two chariots, each drawn by four horses, to pass one another along the top. The Euphrates flowed through the center of the town, and as the river could rise to flood level overnight, the engineers had devised a wonderful system of reservoirs and locks, and a network of canals had been constructed in which the houses were reflected. A wide bridge linked the two halves of the town. Most beautiful of all, however, were the Hanging Gardens of Queen Semiramis. They covered the hillside, one terrace stepped above the other and each supported on pillars— a multistory ornamental park. The soldiers of Alexander's army looked up to the tops of giant trees which had been imported into Babylon from distant lands. Carefully tended and lavishly nurtured by water from the Euphrates, they flourished more vigorously than in their native soil.

Alexander granted his army a long rest. His warriors enjoyed to the full everything they had had to forgo for so long. They drank and feasted until night was turned into day. After fully a month had passed, the clarion calling them to set off once more penetrated their befuddled heads.

26

Alexander Marches to Susa

THE next objectives that Alexander had set himself were Susa and Persepolis, the capitals of the Persian kings.

The satrap of Susa was another of those who came to meet the Macedonians with presents. The most valuable were the white racing dromedaries, capable of running at a fantastic speed. There was also precious water from the river Choaspis, which was as refreshing as spring water from the mountains.

In the treasuries of Susa there were stored bales of purple cloth, and also huge quantities of gold and silver melted down into shapeless lumps. Alexander released all these treasures from their prison houses, and he had coins minted and put into circulation. He sent gifts to Macedonia and Greece, and to all the other countries he now ruled.

Alexander took his seat upon the throne of the Persian emperors, which was so tall that the King's feet did not reach the floor. When Alexander's pages saw this, they ran to get a small low table and they placed it before the throne, so that Alexander could rest his feet on it.

At this, the satrap standing nearby gave a great sigh, and when Alexander asked him the reason for his sorrow, he answered, "King Darius often took his meals from that table, and now his conqueror plants his feet upon it."

Alexander looked thoughtful when he heard this, and he was already giving orders to have the table removed when Philotas cried aloud, "Leave it where it is. You did not know that Darius ate from it, and if his table now serves as your footstool, you may take it as an omen of your firm dominion over his empire."

In Susa Alexander allowed the Persian royal family to return, and he gave the Queen Mother a palace of her own, as was befitting her rank.

A few days before they left for Persepolis, Alexander received a bale of warm woolen material which had been sent him by his own mother, Olympias. It had been brought to Persia by the women who had woven the cloth. As the weather had turned cold, Alexander told these weavers to take a length of the cloth to Sisygambis, and at the same time he suggested that they might teach the daughters of King Darius the art of weaving wool. He was greatly concerned when he learned that Sisygambis had burst into tears at such a proposal, for nothing was more degrading for Persian ladies of high rank than to perform what they considered a menial task.

So Alexander went to see Sisygambis, and pointing to the woolen robe he wore, he said, "Look, Mother. This robe was woven for me by my sister. At home all the women in the royal house occupy themselves with weaving. I meant no insult to you. When I have known what your customs were, I have always respected them. For instance, I know that a son never sits down in his mother's presence until she has given him permission to be seated. That is why I always remain standing before you until you ask me to sit down. And so believe me when I tell you that if I give you a present that my mother sent to me, it is because I wish to honor you as if you too were my mother."

Then Sisygambis thanked him and said, "I have never received a present of greater value."

27

Alexander Sets Fire to the Royal Palace of the Persians

IN the mountains between Susa and Persepolis lived the Uxian people who demanded a toll from all who wished to pass through their territory. When interpreters told them that Alexander, the new Master of the World, was now approaching, they replied, "We have never heard his name. Many a king before him has claimed that he was Master of the World, yet they all paid us what we demand for passage through our country."

And so it came to a battle. The Uxians were soon trapped and they had to yield to Alexander's will. He treated them magnanimously, but he insisted on their paying tribute. Money was quite unknown to these mountain dwellers, and when they offered him sheep and horses instead, Alexander came to terms with them. When all was settled between them, they told him, "Now we know your name. You must indeed be Master of the World if you have conquered even us, the Uxians."

Many of these tribesmen entered the Greek army, which was preparing to march along the great highway to Persepolis.

Alexander himself pressed on into the mountains. He had a small troop with him and he wanted to reach the capital by the shortest route. The satrap of Persepolis advanced to oppose him, for he knew that all was lost if he failed to halt the Macedonian king at this point.

Along the two narrow mountain passes that the people call the Gates of Persia, the rocks on each side are so close together that there is no room for more than two horsemen riding abreast. The satraps had these gateways blocked and walled up with boulders.

But Alexander was not worried. He had had a dream in Babylon in which he was led into Persepolis by a wolf. As he stood before the blocked entrances to the passes, a man came forward and offered to be his guide, and when it turned out that the man's name was Lykos, a word which means "wolf," Alexander put his trust in him implicitly. The "wolf" led the Macedonians by a devious route behind the Persians' backs, and it was the Persians who were caught in an ambush and then routed. Alexander pursued them hotly across the plains in the direction of Persepolis.

The royal palace of the Persians was built on a hill, with a broad flight of steps leading up to it. There were archers carved in stone to accompany the visitor up the stairway, and stone bulls to guard the entrance. In the wall above the flight of stairs, Darius the First had had the following words carved in stone:

> Thus says the king. This land has been given to me to rule by the great god Ahriman. My kingdom is fair, and rich in men and horses. According to the will of the god, and according to my will, it will tremble before no one.

Now soldiers were riding up these steps on horseback. In the forecourt of the palace a statue of King Xerxes was pushed over, so great was the crush. Alexander paused before the fallen image, and when he spoke it seemed as if he were addressing the King himself. "You and your like used big words, but now you lie in the dust," he said. "Do not expect me to set you up again."

And Alexander seated himself on the throne of the Persians, beneath its golden canopy.

A number of Greeks burst into tears of emotion when they saw this. One veteran from Corinth who had lost his father in the war against the Persians cried aloud, "How many Greeks would give their very homes if they could only see this sight—Alexander seated on the throne of the Great King who trampled so many nations in the dust and insulted so many of their gods!"

Then Alexander decided he would give the people a sign that the age of fear was over and that a new era had begun for all the nations. Henceforth there would be no more conquerors and conquered, no more rulers and ruled, but only free people, united in one kingdom. And as Persepolis had been the very hub of the oppressor's empire, Alexander would raze it to the ground.

At a banquet to celebrate the victory, he himself cast a blazing torch and set fire to the cedar paneling that lined the palace walls. The flames devoured the magnificent building—columns, walls and roof alike. The Greeks and Macedonians cheered, but they did not understand what Alexander had intended. They felt that they were the masters now, and they treated the Persians like animals. For fear of the soldiers many of the inhabitants of Persepolis jumped from the walls of the town, and tried to escape into the open country. As soon as Alexander discovered what was happening, he ordered a stop to the persecution. He even had the fire, which he himself had started, extinguished. But at the heart of the Persian empire he left a huge memorial of burnt rubble.

28

Alexander Acquires Vast Treasures

IN the strong rooms of Persepolis and Pasargadä, the neighboring royal palace, they found riches greater even than those
in Babylon and Susa. Alexander divided the spoils lavishly. He
sent home all the Greeks laden with treasure, for now that
their war of vengeance against the Persians was over, he
proposed to press on to the Orient accompanied only by his
Macedonians and the mercenaries.

Alexander showered his Companions and his generals
with gifts until his mother admonished him for his munifi-
cence. To her he sent whole caravans loaded with precious
objects, but she did not want anyone except Alexander and
herself to be rich and powerful.

On one occasion she wrote to him thus:

> Those nearest to you are watching you all the time,
> lusting for gold. And you give it to them in handfuls,
> instead of keeping them in their place. You give them
> so much that they all consider themselves as kings, and
> their arrogance will turn their heads. They will forget
> that everything they have they owe to you and in the
> end they will try to overthrow you—believe me, your
> mother.

Alexander gave this letter to Hephaestion to read. His
friend smiled but Alexander remained serious, and he placed
the seal with which he fastened his letters against Hephaes-

tion's lips. And Hephaestion's mouth remained shut, like a letter that is sealed.

Many of those closest to Alexander did indeed have their heads turned by such unaccustomed wealth. Philotas had sand brought from Egypt so that his wrestlers would fall soft. When he went hunting, he carried so many nets that they would have encircled a city. Others kept a whole retinue of courtiers and personal servants to anoint their bodies.

Alexander chided them for their extravagance. "I am astonished that a few months of living in luxury can have altered you so," he said. "Don't forget that the man who embraces the customs of the conquered has thrown his victory away. It is high time we set off in search of new dangers."

Then Alexander led his army to Ecbatana, the capital of Media. It was there that Darius had fled.

29

Alexander Meets the Dead King of the Persians

THE defeated Persian king gathered together an army for the third time; three thousand cavalry and thirty thousand foot, among them four thousand Greek mercenaries under the leadership of their general, Patron. The Medes and the Bactrian horsemen were under the command of the satraps Bessus and Nabarzanes, who only pretended they were still loyal to the King. In fact, they had conspired to hand Darius over to Alexander, in order to buy the conqueror's favor and to preserve their own rank.

Darius summoned his satraps and commanders and conferred with them. "The gods have turned their faces away from us," said Nabarzanes with hypocritical concern. "Too much misfortune has been heaped upon your head, O Darius. Is it not better in such a case for you to hide yourself away in some secure mountain fastness, and to hand the crown to another man, as if you were dead? Then let your successor advance to fight Alexander in your stead, and if the gods show him greater favor and grant him the victory, it shall be as if it were your victory. You will return to life to terrorize the enemy and will reoccupy the throne. Until then, O King, give your throne to Bessus, as the bravest of us all."

Darius ordered Nabarzanes to be silent and, roused to anger, he turned on the satrap, ready to strike him down with his sword. Bessus threw himself between them and begged forgiveness for Nabarzanes.

Later that evening the Greek general Patron, furious at the double-dealing of the satraps, sought an audience of King Darius to open his eyes to what was going on. Darius understood Greek, and Patron begged the King to give him authority to have Bessus and Nabarzanes put in irons. But Darius said, "If it has come to this, I do not want to be king any longer." And he burst out weeping. The Greek turned away his head and left.

Hardly had he gone when the traitors forced their way into the tent with armed men and laid hands on Darius, who offered no resistance. Before his sovereign's eyes, Bessus rifled the treasure chests that stood in the tent and threw the promised reward to the assassins he had hired. They secured the

King's hands and feet with golden chains and tied him to a bullock cart, hiding their prisoner beneath filthy sheepskins. Then they ordered the cart to be driven away to a remote mountain valley.

Not long after, however, the satraps came chasing after the bullock cart, for news had suddenly reached them that Alexander was approaching. They demanded that Darius should ride with them to meet Alexander and beg for mercy for them all.

Darius refused. He had no wish to live after the humiliation that had been inflicted upon him. So Bessus and Nabarzanes ran him through with their lances. They killed the men they had bribed to murder Darius and also the driver of the cart, who had been utterly bewildered by what was going on. They even stabbed the oxen and they rode off quickly as Macedonian horsemen appeared in the distance.

The lacerated beasts tried to free themselves from the shaft of the cart, but they only succeeded in dragging it over open fields to a spring. There they stopped, tormented by their wounds and by thirst.

Macedonian patrols were searching the countryside, for Darius' interpreter had fallen into their hands, and from him they knew that the King had been tied to a cart and bundled off into the wilds. Therefore everything on wheels was stopped and searched.

Being very thirsty himself, one of these scouts made for the spring to which the suffering oxen had dragged themselves and the wagon. He could see even from a distance that the animals were injured. He galloped up to them and then he saw the figure in the cart, bound and bleeding.

The soldier leaped down from his horse. He pushed aside the soiled pelts and he observed the golden fetters.

"I am Darius," said the dying man.

The Macedonian unfastened the chains and bedded Darius down on the skins. With his helmet he brought him some water from the spring and Darius drank.

"I thank you, foreign soldier," said Darius in Greek. "It is a bitter moment for me, a king, that I have no reward to give you for your kindness to me."

"Alexander, my king, would never have slain you. He will avenge you on your betrayers, of that you can be sure," the Macedonian told him.

Darius tried to raise himself once more. "Tell Alexander that I shall appear before the gods with his name on my lips," he breathed.

And with these words he died.

The horseman kept vigil by the dead King until the other Macedonians caught up to him, and they brought Alexander to the spot as fast as they could.

When Alexander saw Darius, he took off his own cloak and covered the corpse with it. He said nothing, but his men saw the tears that started to his eyes.

Then the rider who had discovered Darius delivered the last message of that unhappy monarch.

"I shall seek out his murderers and avenge him," Alexander promised.

He ordered the body to be embalmed and taken to Persepolis. There Darius would be laid to rest in a royal grave, beside the tombs of earlier Persian kings.

Those who had sought to overthrow Darius were severely punished by Alexander, but those who had remained loyal to their emperor kept their appointments. Their sons were given the command of Persian cavalry squadrons. Then the King absorbed the fighting contingents from all the nations who had paid allegiance to Darius into the Macedonian army. He believed that the time had come to remove the distinctions between the victors and the vanquished. The people everywhere would recognize him as their king.

30

Alexander Demands Obeisance from His Friends, and Sets a Trap for Callisthenes

IT was the custom among the Persians to prostrate themselves before the throne whenever they were received by the King. Having made obeisance, the King would then raise the man in his arms and kiss him like a brother. Alexander now expected his friends to do the same when they appeared before him on ceremonial occasions with the satraps and other high dignitaries.

To get them used to the idea, he gave a banquet to which only Macedonians had been invited. Alexander himself appeared in Persian dress. He stood before his throne, his face radiant. Hephaestion stepped up to him first and bowed low. Alexander lifted him up and kissed him. Then Craterus, Cleitus, Philotas and the other generals approached Alexander, prostrated themselves before him and received his kiss. One by one they knelt, although they all considered it humiliating, or at the least an absurd pantomime.

Only one man refused to bow down before Alexander and that was Callisthenes. He was one of the philosophers who accompanied Alexander on the expedition and, like him, he was a former pupil of Aristotle. Callisthenes greeted the King in the customary Macedonian fashion. Alexander concealed his annoyance with a jest. "You are depriving me of the homage of a scholar, and yourself of a king's kiss."

"Then I must go away a kiss the poorer," replied Callisthenes with a smile. Everyone who heard this admired Callisthenes for his answer, but Alexander never forgave him and from that day on he bore him a deep grudge.

At one particular feast Alexander took it into his head to try to trap Callisthenes. When they were all flushed with wine, and many of them indeed were already drunk, he called on the philosopher to make a speech in praise of the Macedonians.

Callisthenes rose, and did as he was bid without the slightest hesitation. "The Macedonians are an admirable people. They have grown great amid their naked rocks on barren soil. They have absorbed the rugged strength of their mountains, and they have learned to be happy with very little. In this they have proved superior to the Greeks, who are not so easy to please. Since the Macedonians have always been united among themselves they could make the Greeks their brothers and unite with them too. When the time came to wipe out the bitter humiliation that Asia had inflicted on Greece, it was not the Greeks but the Macedonians who took the initiative and led the fight. It was a Macedonian who threw the blazing torch to destroy the palace of the Persian emperors; and the liberated peoples set him upon their throne because he was the worthiest of them all."

His listeners were thrilled by Callisthenes' speech and only Alexander refrained from applause. When the cheering had died down, he said in a sarcastic voice, "It is easy enough to deliver a good speech on a fine subject." Then he challenged Callisthenes to prove his versatility as an orator, this time by holding up a mirror to the Macedonians, so that they could see themselves in it with all their faults, and thus set about correcting them.

Callisthenes looked at Alexander thoughtfully. He could tell that the King no longer trusted him, but he did not allow that to deter him. "The Macedonians are a detestable people," he began. "Compared with the Greeks they are uncouth and incapable of creating beauty. But as they have acquired both the toughness and the insensitivity of the rocks among which they live, they could quickly gain the upper hand over other, more gifted nations. The Macedonians exploited the disunity of the Greeks for their own advantage. On the pretext that they wished to avenge the burning of Greek temples and cities on the Persians, they invaded Asia, and conquered Egypt, Babylon and Persia. They destroyed towns they were incapable of building, and they killed ten times as many people as the population of their own city-state. Not content with that, they are trying to conquer the whole world. The Greeks who advised moderation have been sent home. Macedonians do not keep their word. They say one thing today and something else tomorrow."

"Be silent!" shouted Alexander, white with rage.

"I did as you commanded," replied Callisthenes.

"You have insulted the Macedonians," said Alexander.

"I praised them too," answered Callisthenes. "Every nation deserves both praise and censure. Is there a word I have said that is not true?"

Then Alexander spoke angrily. "As an orator you are incomparable, but you have betrayed your inner feelings. You hate the Macedonians."

"I hate no one," said Callisthenes.

70

31

Alexander Executes Philotas

ONE of his generals who felt particularly humiliated at having to bow before Alexander was Philotas, the son of Parmenion. He was proud of being a Macedonian. It was as a Macedonian that he had fought so bravely—like his father. He was as generous as Alexander himself and had many friends among his own people. As for the other nationalities, Persians and Medes, Bactrians and Parthians, he despised them all. When Alexander put them on an equal footing with his own compatriots, it seemed to Philotas that the King was betraying the Macedonians.

Admittedly it had never occurred to him to raise a revolt against Alexander. But when he was alone among his friends, he gave voice to his thoughts. "Alexander is no longer a Macedonian," he said, "and he will never go home again. The throne of Asia means more to him than the throne of his fathers, and he considers himself a god, so that everything we have done for him counts for little or nothing. My father won victories for his father in many a battle. That counts for nothing. You have all staked your lives a hundred times over for Alexander. That does not count either. Only his deeds count. He did everything, all by himself." That was how Philotas spoke, especially when he was intoxicated. All the same, he never plotted against the King's life.

But there were others who had resolved to kill Alexander, and Philotas found himself involved in the conspiracy. A Macedonian by the name of Limnos started looking around for accomplices among those who were constantly in Alexander's company and he approached one of them, an officer named Nicomachus. But Nicomachus would have nothing to do with treason, and he begged a brother of his to go to Philotas, so that the latter might warn the King. Philotas ignored the warning, and he failed to tell Alexander about the plot, possibly because he did not seriously believe the danger was real and he did not wish to upset the King for nothing. Nicomachos and his brother, however, disclosed the plot to Hephaestion, who immediately had Limnos seized. When he tried to resist arrest, he was killed. At the subsequent investigation, it came to light that Philotas had suppressed the warning he had been given.

Alexander sensed treachery, and he had Philotas brought before a court martial. There the King indicted him in such violent terms that the whole army trembled. In vain Philotas tried to defend himself. Craterus, who was jealous of Philotas, persuaded Alexander to have his rival tortured, and under torture Philotas said anything that was put into his mouth.

The next day Philotas was put to death in the Macedonian fashion. He fell to the ground beneath a hail of spears. The other suspects were executed with him, and in the same way.

32

Alexander Has Parmenion Assassinated

Now that Philotas was dead Alexander grew afraid as he thought of Parmenion, whom he had appointed as governor of the conquered land of Ecbatana. With the death of Philotas, Parmenion had no surviving son, for the two others had fallen in battle, one at Issus and the other at Gaugamela. The imperial treasury was in Parmenion's hands and he was responsible too for the security of all the roads back to Macedonia, as well as having the command of a powerful fighting force. If Parmenion considered that Philotas had been condemned unjustly and led a rebellion, he might well prove more dangerous to Alexander than all his Asiatic enemies.

The King therefore summoned the young cavalry commander, Polydames, and his two brothers. They too had fallen under suspicion, but they had been able to rebut the accusations. Now Alexander turned to Polydames. "In order to show you how much I trust you, I am sending you on a special mission to Ecbatana. You will carry letters to Parmenion, from whom the conspiracy emanated. The night you arrive—and it must be during the hours of darkness—you will go first to my general, Cleander, and hand him a letter. The next morning Cleander will conduct you to Parmenion, who will suspect nothing for he believes you are a friend of his son's, and one of the letters you give to him will be sealed with Philotas' seal." Then turning to the two brothers of Polydames, he told them, "You will both remain as hostages close by my side, until your brother returns from his journey."

With two Arabs for an escort, Polydames set out within the hour. They rode racing camels, for they had to travel across a stretch of desert where there were only a few water holes. During the night of the eleventh day the three riders entered Ectabana, many days before any other messenger could possibly have reached Parmenion with the news of his son's execution.

Polydames went straight to Cleander and handed him the King's letter. Cleander was greatly dismayed, but the next morning, together with two officers whom Alexander had appointed for the deed, he went to the palace to announce the arrival of Polydames to Parmenion.

Parmenion was walking in the park that surrounded the palace. He came forward to meet Polydames and embraced him warmly, because he was the bearer of letters from both his sovereign and his son. As Parmenion broke the seal of the first letter the two officers knocked him to the ground and killed him.

As soon as the deed was known, the soldiers he had commanded started an insurrection, for Parmenion was greatly loved by them all. They pushed their way inside the park, ready to kill Cleander, Polydames and the two officers.

But when Cleander showed them Alexander's letter, the soldiers looked at one another, nonplussed, and they had to withdraw. The King had all the rebels singled out and placed together in one special unit. Here the discipline was so harsh that no one ever again dared to raise his voice against the King.

"And now the murderers of Darius shall be brought to justice," Alexander told his army.

33

Alexander Rests His Horse Bucephalus
and Pardons the Captured Sogdians

AFTER the death of Darius, Bessus had assumed the crown and given himself the title of King Ataxerxes. He thought he was safe from Alexander, for the province where he had taken refuge was virtually inaccessible. Rocky precipices towered to the sky and great stretches of land were covered with waterless desert. In the blazing heat of the sun the air simmered above the burning sand.

These horrors did not deter Alexander from his resolve to track Bessus down. In order to spare Bucephalus he marched on foot at the head of his troops, and everyone could see how he endured the heat and the thirst, while many of his men sank exhausted into the desert sand.

After several days the army came to a mighty river, the Oxus. On a hill by the bank Alexander had a bonfire lighted as a beacon, so that all who were trailing behind could find their way to the camp at night. As at the Danube, Alexander told his men to stuff hides and skins and tie them together to make rafts. Five days later the last man had crossed the Oxus, and the hunt for Bessus continued. Then Alexander received help from an unexpected quarter.

The satrap Spitamenes, who had his eye on the Persian crown himself, conspired with others and they hatched a plot to trap Bessus.

Spitamenes went to him and told him that he had just clapped five conspirators in chains. Bessus had the captives brought in and he was about to kill the traitors with his own hand, when all five flung off their shackles. Bessus, paralyzed for a moment by such unexpected deception, was overpowered. Spitamenes handed him over to Alexander who had him executed for regicide. This, however, did not put an end to all Persian resistance.

The upland valleys were ruled over by princes who were not prepared to transfer their allegiance to Alexander. They rode agile mountain ponies and could deploy troops of highly mobile cavalry, against which a great army was helpless. So Alexander mounted his soldiers on native Sogdian horses, and he himself rode a horse that had been bred in this wild country when he went out on punitive expeditions. Bucephalus was led along with the baggage train.

One day, however, the baggage train was ambushed, and when the enemy made off with their booty, they took Bucephalus with them. The moment Alexander heard of what had happened, he set off in pursuit. The robbers had taken refuge in their fortress and they were confident that their walls were strong enough to resist invaders. When Alexander demanded the return of his horse, they only jeered in reply.

Thereupon Alexander had the following message sent to them:

> Alexander has never allowed a fortress to go unconquered, not even one on an island in the midst of the sea. If you do not give him back his charger, not a stone of your citadel will remain standing. The land will be laid waste for miles around, and he will turn you into a feast of carrion for the vultures. But if you return Alexander's black horse with the white blaze on its forehead, he will reward you.

At this, the gates of the fortress were opened, and a little cavalcade started down from the mountain citadel, led by Bucephalus. Alexander advanced to meet the procession and Bucephalus at once broke into a trot. The men who had kidnaped the horse cheered loudly when they saw how rapturously Alexander and Bucephalus greeted one another. "A king like that is one we would be proud to serve," said their leader.

Then the other Sodgians, who had submitted to Alexander only after bitter fighting, all said the same.

"You must die," Alexander told them. "Five times you refused to open the gates of your fortress to me."

The Macedonians stepped forward to shackle them but the Sogdians protested with one voice. "We are not afraid of death," they said, "but we have not deserved the indignity of these fetters."

So the King gave orders for them to be led away unbound to their execution and the Sogdians marched off, singing.

Alexander was astonished. Did they not know they were being led to their deaths, they were asked.

Then one of the condemned men spoke. "For us, to die means that we are being sent to join our ancestors. That is one reason for rejoicing. We have another reason too. Is it not the conqueror of all the nations, the master of the world, who is sending us on this journey?"

On hearing this, Alexander could not find it in his heart to have them executed and instead he enrolled them in his army.

34

Alexander Conquers a Mountain Eyrie and Marries Roxana

MORE Macedonians were killed in these skirmishes in Sogdiana than in all the great battles, and yet Alexander refused to leave this inhospitable country beneath the roof of the world until the last mountain eyrie had been subdued. He pressed on, climbing to heights that are covered with ice and snow the whole year round. Many a sentry froze at his post and made no answer when the relief guard arrived and gave the password. The cold was their most dangerous enemy, for no armor could protect them against it. Alexander had fires lighted whenever wood could be found, and soldiers and horses flocked around the blaze.

On one occasion, an elderly soldier suffering from snowblindness was led up to the fire. Alexander stood up when he saw the old man, made him sit down on his throne and gave him mulled wine to drink—all without saying a word. Stimulated by the fire and the wine, the old soldier began complaining loudly. "What kind of war is this we are supposed to be fighting, a war against frozen mountains? Which of us has anything to gain here, except that fellow Alexander who is never satisfied?"

At that moment his eyes opened, and he saw who it was standing by his side and holding his arm so that he would not fall into the fire. And when he realized that he was sitting on the King's throne, panic-stricken he tried to rise.

"Stay where you are, old man," Alexander reassured

him. "You are sitting on Alexander's throne, not Darius'. Whatever is mine belongs to you all."

The last of the Sogdian princes to keep up his resistance was called Ariamazes. His castle topped a mountain that fell away in sheer cliffs on three sides, while a steep and narrow path led up the fourth side to the gates of the citadel. Towering above it was a spur of rock. Alexander demanded that Ariamazes hand over his castle, and everyone inside was promised safe conduct.

Ariamazes retorted that the King had better find himself soldiers with wings if he wanted to take the fortress. For ordinary human beings, even for Macedonians, it was impregnable, he declared.

But Alexander's pride would not allow him to leave the castle unconquered. He had announced throughout the camp that anyone who climbed the rock which dominated the fortress would be rewarded with a talent of silver.

Three hundred men volunteered. They were experienced climbers from the mountains of Macedonia and they burned to distinguish themselves in the eyes of the King.

As soon as night fell, the men took iron spikes, hammers and ropes and the great enterprise began. The rest of the army set up a wild hullabaloo around their campfires, so that the enemy would not notice what was happening.

The sheer mountain face was covered with ice, and thirty of the climbers fell into the abyss to their deaths. But by the first light of dawn the remainder had scaled to the topmost pinnacle of rock that overlooked the fortress. They had climbed with flags wrapped around their bodies and these they unwound at the summit. In the early morning breeze, the banners floated like huge wings above their shoulders.

Then Alexander had word sent to Ariamazes that he had found his winged soldiers, and when the Sogdians looked up, they were aghast to see the Macedonians silhouetted against the sky line. Thereupon Ariamazes opened the castle gates.

The besieged citizens feared that they would be punished severely because they had held out so long. But nothing of the sort happened. One of those who had remained in the fortress was Roxana, a daughter of Ariamazes. Fascinated by her beauty, Alexander decided to make her his wife.

The wedding took place in the palace immediately. In order to show everybody that all hatred was at an end, the conqueror married the daughter of his enemy according to Iranian custom. A loaf of bread was handed to him and he cut it in two with his sword and gave half to Roxana.

Ariamazes, together with his warriors, entered Alexander's service. Other Sogdian princes followed his example. And when the corrupt Spitamenes was betrayed in his turn as Bessus had been, Alexander became the undisputed ruler of the whole Persian Empire.

35

Alexander Kills Cleitus

THE two provinces for which Alexander had had to fight the hardest he gave to Cleitus, who had saved his life at the Battle of the Granicus. In Marakanda he appointed him to be governor of Bactria and Sogdiana.

On the evening of the appointment, the King invited his friends to a banquet in honor of Cleitus. Fruit from Macedonia had been specially imported for the feast, and Alexander had it ready for his guests.

Soon the feasting grew noisy and everyone drank heavily. Minstrels were sent for and they sang satirical songs, making fun particularly of the oldest of Alexander's Macedonian Companions; like the others, Cleitus was one of their butts.

One of the balladmongers was so bold as to poke fun at Philip, Alexander's father. He sang a song that went like this:

> At Chaeronea, the blood ran red.
> Philip was frightened and soon shammed dead.
> But Alexander plunged into the fray,
> Alone, unaided, he saved the day!

Cleitus jumped to his feet and asked Alexander if such a lie were not too much even for his ears. The King behaved as if he had not heard.

Then Cleitus began declaiming a passage from a Greek tragedy:

> Alas! In Greece how ill the custom runs
> The trophies stand inscribed with names of kings,
> The blood that won the field was other men's!

"Enough!" shouted Alexander. "Be silent!"

"Too many are silent already!" roared Cleitus. "Parmenion is silent, the man who won so many victories for you and for your father! Must I be silent too, I whom you have to thank that you are still alive today?"

Alexander sprang to his feet and bombarded Cleitus with apples. The fruit bounced off his face, but Cleitus went on speaking. "Listen, Alexander! For once you shall hear the truth. We who have marched with you from the very beginning of the campaign can find no joy in it any longer. How much happier are they who fell in battle than those of us who are here today. They do not have to ask the Persians for permission to enter your presence!" By now all the Macedonian guests were on their feet, trying to pacify Cleitus, but he had not had his say yet. "From now on, do not invite free men to your table," he cried, "but only those who are willing to bow down before you."

Alexander was beside himself with rage and his hand flew to his sword, but the captain of the guard had removed it in good time. The King called for his pages to bring his weapons, and he ordered the trumpeter to sound the alarm which would summon all the Macedonians in camp to arms. The trumpeter refused. Alexander struck him in the face with his fist, but the trumpeter would not budge. Meanwhile, Cleitus had been dragged out of the tent by his friends.

But he pushed his way in again through another entrance, and one that was nearer to Alexander this time.

" 'Alas! In Greece how ill the custom runs . . . .' " he repeated at the top of his voice.

Alexander, maddened with fury, snatched a spear from his bodyguard and ran Cleitus through the body. Then, horrified at what he had done, he wrenched the spear from the wound and tried to kill himself with it. His friends snatched it away and broke it in pieces. Alexander threw himself over the corpse of Cleitus, and for three days his friends had to keep watch over him, to see that he did not kill himself.

In the end, it was the seer Aristander who was able to restore the King to his senses. Three days before the terrible deed Alexander had told him that he had had a dream in

82

which he saw Cleitus sitting among the sons of Parmenion, but they were all dead men.

"They have called Cleitus to them," said Aristander. "But you are called by the land from whose peaks you will see the eastern rim of the world."

These words of Aristander's comforted the King and consoled him in his grief.

36

Alexander Burns the Baggage Carts

ALEXANDER had dreamed of India since the days of his boyhood when he had first won Bucephalus. In that year a parrot had been brought from India to the royal court at Pella. The parrot spoke a few words of an Indian language, and Aristotle had taught him some Greek. The King, the Queen, Alexander, indeed the whole court, had gathered around the bird, whose feathers were of brighter hue than the robes of the Persian ambassadors.

In the army with which Alexander set out for India there were many nationalities serving. There were Persians and Parthians, Iranians, Bactrians, Sogdians and Scythians, Mardi, Dahai and Massegetae—the army was as colorful as the parrot's feathers. The core of the army consisted of the Macedonians, with whom Alexander had begun his campaign seven years before.

Alexander was accompanied by Roxana, and a number of princes traveling with the army also had their wives with them, as did many of the soldiers. The baggage train was enormous and there were countless wagons laden with the spoils of war.

Alexander knew that there were mountains ahead of them through which there would be no roads for such heavily laden carts, so he had all the ones that carried booty un-hitched, his own included. Then he turned to the army. "Let us now make a sacrifice to the gods and burn all the plunder we have taken. We shall not be the losers thereby, for in return the gods will give us lands that are as rich in marvels as they are in treasure."

At this the Macedonians began to murmur. But when Alexander thrust a burning torch into his own wagon, and his generals followed suit so that a great flame flared toward the sky, then a wave of enthusiasm gripped the soldiers. They cast their spoils into the fire with their own hands and called on Alexander to lead them into India.

37

Alexander Marches to India

THE deeper the Macedonians penetrated into the country, the greater was their amazement. Everything was different from what they were accustomed to—the animals, the vegetation and the people. They saw trees with aerial roots, and once they came to a forest of tall stalks on which hung little half-moons that could be eaten when the yellow shell was removed.

Soon there was bitter fighting. The Indians from the mountains defended themselves desperately and Alexander was wounded.

He divided the army and sent one half on ahead under the command of Hephaestion and Perdiccas. Their orders were to build a bridge over the river Indus. Alexander himself would subdue the mountain tribes. He always led the way with a small advance party, and he was always the first to attack.

On one occasion the Macedonians pitched their camp at night. They did not know that the town of Mysa was close by, and the Mysans were similarly unsuspecting, for a forest separated the camp from the city.

As it was cold, the Macedonians collected big bundles of wood and set them aflame, but the trees themselves caught fire. The Mysans were awakened by the brightness of the glow and the crackling of the flames. With horror they saw a wall of fire coming toward them, and it was only then, when they heard loud screams and the barking of dogs, that the Macedonians discovered how close to a town they had camped. If only the inhabitants of Mysa had been more vigilant, they could easily have fallen upon Alexander's army and destroyed it.

The most violent fighting took place around the rock of Aornos. This pinnacle of living rock is cut off from the rest of the mountains by a deep gorge. Its name means "Without birds," and suggests that even the birds would find it difficult to infiltrate the citadel that crowns the peak. Not even winged soldiers would have helped here.

Every assault on the narrow path that led to the gates was beaten off. Then Alexander had a whole forest felled. Boulders, rocks and tree trunks were rolled down into the ravine until it was filled to ground level. After seven days, when the defenders saw wooden siege towers advancing toward their citadel and threatening a direct attack, they surrendered.

Alexander invited them to his table and it was there that the chieftain, flushed with wine, told him a story.

"The rock of Aornos was besieged once before by a Greek, in ancient times, and his name was Herakles. He was a hero who accomplished great deeds, but he could not conquer Aornos, though the earth itself came to his aid and trembled in an attempt to shatter the rock. But it stood firm like the courage of its defenders, and Herakles had to go away, thwarted."

In return for his tale, Alexander made the Indian a present of his sword; but he also built an altar to appease Herakles, in case the god was offended.

38

Alexander Meets King Taxiles

IT took Alexander sixteen days to reach the Indus from the rock of Aornos. Hephaestion had had a bridge built across the river and now the whole army marched over it. The king of the land on the far side was called Taxiles. He was Taxiles the One Hundred and Fourth, for every ruler assumed the same name on his accession and so it was said that Taxiles had reigned since the beginning of time.

This monarch advanced to meet Alexander, followed by his whole army. He had war elephants in his retinue and from afar, it looked as if gray towers were moving toward them in the midst of the soldiers. This martial appearance roused Alexander's suspicions. He told his army to halt and he drew them up in battle order. As soon as Taxiles saw the Macedonians pause, he too brought his army to a standstill. Then he rode forward, alone.

Alexander felt that he was being challenged to a duel and he rode toward Taxiles. Thus the two kings met in the no man's land between their armies. But instead of reaching for his weapons, Taxiles stretched out his right hand in friendship and Alexander grasped it. Then the Indian king made Alexander a present of fifty-six elephants.

Alexander was surprised at the enormous fighting strength that the Indian could muster, and he asked him if he had not more soldiers than peasants.

"As I am threatened by powerful enemies, many of my peasants have had to become soldiers," Taxiles replied.

"They will soon return to their fields," Alexander promised him, "for now we can go forward as allies and take the field against your antagonists."

He then asked Taxiles what was the name of his strongest enemy. "He is called Porus," said Taxiles, "and he is a giant in every respect—in stature, in intellect and in courage. He rides an elephant and his kingdom lies on the opposite bank of the Hydaspes."

"Then we shall advance against him right away," said Alexander.

39

Alexander Defeats King Porus

AFTER the melting of the snows and heavy cloudbursts, the Hydaspes had become a raging torrent. It roared past Alexander and his army. On the far bank stood a mighty wall of men, above which loomed two hundred gray turrets, the war elephants of King Porus. Alexander saw that it was impossible to cross the river at this point. So he thought out a stratagem.

Day after day a great noise arose from the camp, until the sentries of King Porus grew quite used to it. One night, when the rain was pouring down in torrents, Alexander moved upstream along the river bank with five thousand cavalry and six thousand infantrymen, until he reached a spot opposite an island in the river. From the dense low clouds the lightning flashed, and twelve horsemen and four foot soldiers were struck by its burning spears. It also felled a tree by which Alexander was standing. The river overflowed its banks and carried away rafts and tree trunks with soldiers clinging to them, so that they were drowned and so were some of the horses. But at last the opposite bank was reached and Alexander allowed his men to rest until daybreak. Then he marched them downstream. King Porus, sensing the danger, had sent out a troop of horses led by his own son to reconnoiter. There was a skirmish, and the prince and many Indian horsemen with him lost their lives. Those who escaped brought the news that Alexander was advancing.

Porus prepared for battle. He deployed his troops on a

broad front. Three hundred fighting chariots covered the flanks, and next to them the cavalry closed in. The infantry were drawn up in the center, with one hundred men behind each of the elephants.

Alexander pierced the left flank of the Indian army with his cavalry, and he dealt them such a blow that riders and chariots fled. The Macedonian javelin throwers advanced against the center where Porus was enthroned on his elephant and the Macedonian archers shot at the elephants with a hail of arrows. The wounded animals turned to flee, trampling down everything that stood in their path. The mighty Porus fought to the end, flinging spear after spear into the enemy's ranks. When he had no more weapons left, he gave his elephant the signal to go down on its knees. The King dismounted and collapsed. The elephant remained kneeling by its master's side and it was trying to pull an arrow out of the King's shoulder with its trunk when Alexander arrived on the scene. He came on foot, for Bucephalus had been slain in the fight. The Indian king's elephant also died on the battlefield, but Porus himself recovered from his wounds. When Alexander asked Porus how he should be treated, Porus answered, "Like a king."

So Alexander allowed him to keep his kingdom and he even added more land to it. He reconciled Porus and Taxiles, and thus an old feud was ended.

Alexander had a town built on the spot where Bucephalus had met his death, and he named it after his horse.

40

Alexander Learns a Lesson from King Dindimus

FROM Porus and Taxiles, Alexander learned that there were other kings in the great land of India, as many kings as there were rivers. These rivers were broad, and the kings were powerful. "They all have war chariots and war elephants like mine," said Porus. "The next river you will come to is the Hyphasis."

Then Alexander took leave of the King in order to continue on his way to the east.

Soon the spies he had sent ahead returned to Alexander and said, "We have found a king who lives in the forest. His name is Dindimus and he has neither war chariots nor fighting elephants. He has no house and he is dressed in humble fashion. He lives alone and he is a man of great dignity."

"Then bring me this forest king," commanded Alexander. "I wish to see him and speak to him."

"We wanted to bring him," said the scouts, "but he would not come with us. We threatened him, yet he showed no fear."

Then Alexander told them to take him to Dindimus.

Dindimus sat under a tree on the bare earth, wearing a simple garment. He invited Alexander to sit down with him, but Alexander remained standing and said mockingly, "Where is your house, King Dindimus?"

Dindimus pointed to the tree under which he sat.

"And where is your table, King Dindimus?"

Dindimus pointed to the ground in front of him where there stood a dish of fruit and a jug of water.

"And where is your kingdom, King Dindimus?"

"The sun that shines on us all, the air we all breathe, the earth we can all see is my kingdom," answered Dindimus. "What more do I need?"

Alexander, who had conquered so many countries, was growing impatient. "How can you call yourself a king when you have no power?" he asked.

"I had power once," replied Dindimus. "My father bequeathed me a great army. I sent all the soldiers home so that they could till the fields."

"And who will guard you if someone comes and threatens you?" said Alexander.

"Why should anyone threaten me?" asked Dindimus in turn. "My possessions are fewer than anyone else's. Therefore I sleep soundly and when I wake I have no cares."

Then Alexander thought of the wise Diogenes, whom he had met in Corinth and he did not mock Dindimus any more.

"I must leave you now," said Alexander, "for I have still a long way to travel."

"Where are you going?" asked Dindimus.

"To the end of the world," answered Alexander.

Dindimus looked up at the King, puzzled. "But why are you in such a hurry? We all get there one day."

41

Alexander Attacks at the Edge of the Forest

ONE day, when Alexander was out on reconnaissance with only a few of his men, he saw a long row of shadowy figures lurking on the outskirts of a forest. He called a halt immediately. His soldiers too could see the cowering figures, and Alexander gave the signal to attack. With their lances held high above their heads, the Macedonian horsemen galloped toward the leafy woods.

All at once the trees began to sway, for as the attack got under way, the mysterious forms swarmed up the trunks in frantic haste and perched among the treetops. The branches whipped up and down like the beating of wings.

When the Macedonians were close enough to see the situation properly, some of them laughed so hard that they fell off their horses. These were no Indian warriors whom they had startled and put to flight but a troop of monkeys. There were over one hundred of them, grinning down at the Macedonians from the leafy crowns of the trees.

Alexander turned back with his horsemen, and the whole camp rocked with laughter when they heard the story of the battle of the monkeys.

42

Alexander Turns Back

THE very next day Alexander issued orders to advance. The army was dismayed at his impatience, for by now the men were growing exhausted and it was a great effort for them even to drag themselves from one camp to the next. Many of the soldiers were sick, too. True, there were no more enemy armies blocking their path, but the rains had set in and it had not stopped pouring now for seventy days! Much of the territory they had to cross was swarming with snakes whose bite was fatal. The army's equipment was rotting and their clothes hung in rags. When the Macedonians reached the river Hyphasis, they could not see the opposite bank.

Alexander's Companions looked out over the water and one of them said, "This is the end of the world."

An Indian prince arrived at the camp to offer Alexander his allegiance and to give him presents. "The end of the world is still a long way off," this prince told them. "The land beyond the Hyphasis is a vast wilderness, and it will take you twelve days to march across it. Then you will reach the Ganges, which is the mightiest river in all of India, with wealthy nations living along its banks. Their kings are warriors and one of them, Agrames, commands six thousand fighting elephants."

"A number has never frightened us yet," said Alexander lightly. "We are used to defeating armies of elephants."

He told his men to build rafts, so that they might cross the Hyphasis in a week.

Toward evening the cloud cover lifted and the following day the air was as clear as glass. In the northeast glistened the Himalaya Mountains, an insurmountable wall.

The whole army was horrified when they heard Alexander's latest command to cross the river. They mustered outside the tent of their king and they waited in silence until Alexander appeared. He looked at the men gathered there and his face was a mask. Then he broke the stillness. "Well, what is it?" he demanded.

As no one answered him, Alexander spoke again. "I know what you want but I cannot do it. Go back to your tents."

No one moved.

"Well then, say something at least, so that I do not stand here helplessly like a man lost in the desert," he insisted. He went up to Coenus, a general whom he had promoted from the ranks during the course of the campaign, and he shook him roughly. "Don't stand there like a stone," he said. "Speak up if you have anything to say to me."

Then Coenus began. "I do not speak for myself alone. All of us who stand here before you have only one request: lead us home. It is eight years since we have seen our homeland. These foreign lands are swallowing us up. They are making us ill. Have we not fought enough battles for you, won enough victories, crossed enough rivers, stormed enough mountain fortresses? Have you not fulfilled your task and avenged Greece on the Persians? Is it not enough for you that you are Pharaoh of Egypt and Great King of Asia? Does the rest of the world appeal to you with a louder voice than the land that bore you—and us?" And pointing to the Himalayas, he cried, "Is the call of this wall of rock and ice stronger than the call of the mountains of Macedonia?"

94

"I have never forgotten Macedonia," replied Alexander.
"We shall return there, I promise you. But why do you want
to turn back now, only one step from our goal? Why do you
want to cheat me, and yourselves too, out of our last victory?"

Then a common soldier stepped forward. "Look at us!"
he said. "We are dead men, worse than corpses. If you want
us to carry out your commands, you must breathe new life
into us. What does one more victory mean to us after so
many conquests? I do not want to dip this hand of mine in
blood again, but only in the cool water of the well before
my house." He stretched out his hand toward the army. "That
is what we all want."

Then the thousands who stood before the King, ragged
and pale, broke into weeping. Alexander turned away, and
went back into his tent.

No one dared to go in to him. On the third day, however, he sent for Hephaestion, who took him a message from
Aristander. The seer told Alexander this: "The gods expect
us to go back. Dionysus feels offended because someone else
has penetrated deeper into India than he."

When he heard these words, Alexander had the army
informed of the oracle. There was such jubilation at this pro-
nouncement that Alexander grew afraid. Some soldiers were
so carried away with joy that they rushed into his tent and
brought him out into the midst of his army. Many of the
men tried to clasp his hand and Coenus, who had spoken out
three days before, was once again the army's spokesman. "We
will follow you on a second great expedition, even if it takes
us to the Pillars of Herakles."

On the river bank Alexander had twelve high altars
erected, a tower for every Greek god. He also founded a
town there with his name and called it Alexandria the

95

Farthest. On that day, Callisthenes said to Alexander, "I believed you were capable of any victory except this last. Now that you have won it, all who doubted you must feel ashamed, myself included."

In torrential rain, the army set out on the march back to the Hydaspes.

43

Alexander Travels Down the Indus

ON the banks of the Hydaspes, Alexander allowed his army to rest for two whole months. There was much speculation, however, when Craterus took a party of soldiers and natives into the foothills of the Himalayas and returned with thousands of tree trunks. With this timber a fleet was built— eighty large galleys constructed as floating fortresses, as well as two hundred transport canoes for carrying men, horses, provisions and weapons. More than one thousand other craft were bought or commandeered. Cretans, Egyptians, Carians, Phoenicians and Greeks from the archipelago who had traveled with the baggage train made up the crews of these vessels, for Alexander was determined to explore the seas to the south of India.

At the beginning of November, there began a river procession of unprecedented splendor. A moving range of hills accompanied the boats on both banks of the river—the two hundred elephants that Alexander had received as presents from the Indian kings and princes. They were draped in cloth of purple and their heads were decked with nodding tufts of feathers. Behind them, in mighty columns, marched the main body of the army, one column led by Hephaestion and the other by Craterus.

At sunrise after a solemn sacrifice, Alexander, his nearest Companions, the cavalry and the archers embarked on the ships which were rigged with sails of every hue. The rhythmic calls of the rowers alternated with the folk songs of the various tribes and peoples. Indians came flocking down to the river from the forests and traveled part of the way with them. They made music on drums and flutes, and when the soldiers rested there were dancers to entertain them. This carnival along the river and its banks lasted for several weeks. Everyone was in high spirits, Alexander included. Once he said, "Dionysus, the god of merrymaking, is traveling through India for the second time. It is he who is leading our expedition."

As the fleet neared the confluence of the Hydaspes and the Acesines, which is the middle branch of the Five Rivers, the great festival came to a sudden end. The boats were seized by rapids and whirlpools which pounded them and drove them into collision with one another. For the joining of the rivers throws up a tidal bore, and there are mudbanks lurking in the troubled waters.

Hastily the sails were reefed, for by now the wind had sprung up too and it buffeted the fleet with violent gusts. In the furious current two large boats collided and more than thirty of the smaller ones capsized and sank. The ship on which Alexander was traveling was one of those seized by a whirlpool. The steering broke and the vessel spun around in circles, helpless in the seething waters. Alexander dived over-board and tried to reach the bank and safety. The little boats hastened to his aid.

He was as pale as a corpse when he was dragged out of the water at last and hauled aboard one of the boats. By the time he had recovered from his dead faint, the fleet was out of danger too. The damage was quickly repaired.

At the confluence of these rivers, Alexander had two altars built. The waters played no more tricks on the fleet, and bore the ships safely southward toward the open sea.

44

Alexander Risks His Life in the Fortress of the Mallians

BUT now warlike tribes barred the way. These tribes pos-sessed fortified towns and large armies and they put an end to the feuds among themselves in order to fight Alexander's army. They had already assembled sixty thousand soldiers, twelve thousand cavalry and eight hundred war chariots, when their princes started quarreling among themselves over who should be the commander-in-chief, and each of them took umbrage and withdrew his soldiers. There was hard fighting against certain of these tribes, however, especially the Mallians. Alexander advanced against them across an arid stretch of desert and he conquered several of their towns. But many of their soldiers fled and took refuge in their capi-tal, which was guarded by their best troops.

Alexander was exasperated because this fighting was delaying his journey to the sea. He had the walls sapped and battering-rams brought up before the gates of the city. Scaling ladders were placed on three sides and flaming torches were flung from the boats and into the town. One of the gates was torn from its hinges, and the Macedonians pushed their way inside.

But still the fortress would not surrender. The wall was built on rock and its gate was armored. The Macedonians were bombarded with arrows and spears. Alexander worked himself up into a fury and called for ladders to hook over the top of the wall. Covered by hundreds of his archers, he and three Companions, Peucestas, Leonnatus and Abreas, succeeded in climbing to the top of the wall. But once they were up, they realized that they were completely exposed to a storm of arrows and they themselves could not retaliate. Alexander did not hesitate. He jumped down from the wall into the citadel, into the very heart of the melee. The Mallians were taken aback. Then they rallied and pressed forward, closing in on the solitary figure in the burnished helmet. Alexander ran three of his assailants through with his sword. The Mallian archers kept up a volley of arrows and Alexander, hard pressed, felt his shield grow heavy. Then the Companions jumped down too. Abreas was killed immediately and a moment later an arrow hit Alexander, piercing deep into his breast. Peucestas managed to cover the King with his shield until further help arrived.

The city was taken but Alexander had to be carried out on his shield. The army stood and watched in profound silence. Everyone thought that Alexander was dead. But when the arrow was pulled out of the wound, the pain brought the King to his senses again. He had himself carried to his ship so that all could see him, and a great wave of cheering broke out when he waved his hand. The soldiers thronged to the bank, threw their helmets in the air and brandished their shields and weapons.

Four days later, when Alexander crossed a bridge of ships to dry land, he did not need any support. And when he actually mounted his horse again, the hills echoed with shouts of joy. Everyone wanted to be close to their king and to receive his glance. Their faces shone with tears of happiness.

45

Alexander Questions the Captured Brahmins

THE winter camp was pitched in the kingdom of Musicanus. There Alexander was able to recover from his grievous wounds, and he celebrated his return to health with sacrifices to the gods and with solemn games.

The country was quiet at first, but then the Brahmins began stirring up a revolt. Five of the ringleaders were taken prisoner and brought before Alexander for sentence.

"You all deserve to die," he said, "for many people have lost their lives as a result of your inflammatory speeches. Yet you claim to be men of great wisdom, so I will put you to the test. I will ask each of you a question, and anyone who answers badly shall be put to death." Then turning to the first captive, he asked, "Which of all the animals in the world is the most cunning?"

"An animal not yet known to man," said the Brahmin, and the King gave him his freedom.

"Which is stronger, rock or water?" he asked the second prisoner.

"Water," was the reply, "for it gnaws its way through rock and can even split it when it turns to ice."

Alexander released him too and then he asked the third Brahmin, "Which came first, day or night?"

"Night," answered the third man, "for the day had first to sleep before it could wake up." And he too was freed.

The fourth question was this. "Which can see more, the eye of a man or the mind?"

"The mind," said the fourth Brahmin, "for with his mind, a man can even see around corners."

Then Alexander laughed. "I like your answer so much that I will grant a pardon to two of you in return for it." And so the fifth Brahmin also had his shackles removed. Alexander allowed them all to go free, but warned them that in the future they should promote peace and not war.

The fifth of these wise men was named Calanus. He was very old and he said to Alexander, "I am especially indebted to you because you spared me the ordeal of an answer. If you approve, therefore, I will go with you for part of your way."

This suggestion pleased the King, and Calanus remained in his train as one of his followers. He was allowed to travel on board the ship that carried Alexander.

46

Alexander Sails Out to Sea

DURING his winter encampment, Alexander had so many ships built that half his army could sail down the Indus to the point where the river divides into two arms. There lay the city of Patala.

From here Alexander set sail with five ships down the western branch of the Indus, in order to explore the ocean, which was believed to gird the whole earth with its waters.

Strangely enough, the fishermen who lived in the villages by the river's edge knew nothing of the sea. But Alexander's helmsmen said that they could already smell the salt in the air.

At last they came to a village whose inhabitants told them that a day's journey further the river became bitter to drink.

And so it proved. On the following day when they drew water from the Indus, it tasted salty. Presently they noticed too that the current was flowing in the opposite direction.

Alexander told his men to moor the ships to the bank. He and his Companions went ashore to look for pilots, but they could find no one. They were horrified when they came back after a long search to discover that their ships were grounded, and reared high above the surface of the shallow water.

A night passed in fear and doubt but the next morning the river began to rise again. It rose with such force that the ships were thrown against one another. In this way the

Macedonians learned about the ebb and flow of the tide.

Before the water level fell again, Alexander steered his ship out to the open sea, close to an offshore island. It was a barren isle, on which grew neither tree nor shrub. From here Alexander continued southward until he could see nothing but water and sky. Then he cast gifts into the sea as a sacrifice and he thanked the gods for fulfilling his dearest wish— to sail out beyond the rim of the world.

It was now that Alexander turned his thoughts to returning home at last. He decided that a small section of the army would go by sea from the mouth of the Indus to the Euphrates. There were enough ships and enough seamen to sail them, but he still had to find the right man to be Admiral of the Fleet. He conferred with his closest friends, Hephaestion and Nearchus.

"All our Macedonians have shown their courage on land," said Alexander, "but what will happen if there are storms at sea? Whom would they trust most?"

"Give me the command," said Nearchus.

"I would never place one of my closest Companions in such great peril," replied Alexander.

"That is the only way you will give the men confidence for the voyage," argued Nearchus, "and who is more fitted for the task than I? I come from Crete, and I have been familiar with the sea since childhood. The god of the sea will not harm us, for neither you nor I have ever offended him."

Then Alexander named Nearchus as his Admiral of the Fleet. The news reassured the ships' crews as much as if Alexander himself had assumed the command. Now the vessels were enthusiastically prepared for the voyage along the coast, and they were decorated as if for a festival. Every captain tried to get the best seamen for his crew, and so great was the enthusiasm that officers and men alike wanted to put to sea at once.

But it happened to be the monsoon season, and the wind from the open sea blew so strongly that it was impossible to sail. According to the Indians, it was only at the end of September that the winds would change. Until then the fleet would have to remain at anchor in the waters of the Indus.

47

Alexander Leads His Army Through the Gedrosian Desert

ALEXANDER marched into the Gedrosian Desert with one hundred thousand men. Something drove him to attempt this feat, one that had never been dared before, except by Queen Semiramis of Babylon and the Persian king Cyrus. Both armies, the Babylonian and the Persian alike, had perished in the desert.

The villages at the edge of the wilderness had been abandoned. The inhabitants had crept into hiding before the advancing Macedonians, but the landscape welcomed the infiltrators with trees of myrrh in bloom. The merchants with the baggage train collected the precious sap that ran down the trunks. The large blossoms were trampled underfoot by soldiers and animals too, and they gave out an intoxicating perfume. Soon, however, the myrrh yielded to thornbushes, through which the soldiers had to hack their way with their swords. Then the desert proper stretched out before them, a waste of sand littered with stones.

The army marched southwest, toward the coast. They had to dig wells for the fleet and leave stores of food for them. There was no water to be found anywhere. All the rivers had dried up, and the pebbles in the stream beds were burning hot to the touch.

But one day a dead river was turned into a roaring torrent in a matter of minutes. It was high noon and the army was resting along the river bed. The horses and pack animals sniffed the danger first and tried to bolt. Then the soldiers had to run for their lives as a great tidal wave came racing down on them with an uncanny rushing noise. The Macedonians used helmets or anything else that came to hand to catch the water, but these containers were swept away. After three hours the spell was lifted and the river bed glowed with heat once more.

From then on Alexander chose the shortest possible route through the desert, and natives guided the army from one water hole to the next. By day men and beasts sought shelter from the murderous glare of the sun and stayed in their tents when they could, or under awnings of blankets. By night they marched, and the desert sand shone like silver in the light of the stars and the moon.

Supplies grew short. The cavalry slaughtered one horse after another and before long the pack animals had to be killed too. The guards themselves broke into the wagons where corn and dates had been packed under lock and key, to be used only in the most dire emergency. They were not punished, however, for the situation was indeed desperate by then. One by one they staggered through the deep sand, sinking into it at every step. Many remained where they fell, lying among the dunes, and none of those still plodding on turned his head to spare them a glance. No one who lagged behind could hope to reach the next water hole.

Sandstorms had obliterated the landmarks and signposts and on many nights the guides themselves went astray. Then the company had to march by day after all, and to breathe the scorching air that seared their lungs. Their eyes grew bloodshot, and the soldiers threw away their weapons. Some imagined they could see pools of water in the distance, and they ran toward them until their feet could not carry them any further. Others went out of their minds with fear, because they saw giant snakes and scorpions coming to attack them.

Once one of the patrols found an unexpected trickle of water and they filled a helmet and took it to Alexander. The King looked around at his men, watching him. He refused to drink and poured the water into the sand.

After sixty days the end of the desert was reached. In those two months Alexander had lost more men than in the nine years of his campaign from Macedonia to the Indus. In Pura, the capital of Carmania, the greatly depleted army reassembled and Alexander marched them on to the west. He wanted to reach the coast, for he had heard nothing of Nearchus and the fleet for a long time and he feared for their safety.

48

Alexander Has a Search Made for Nearchus and the Fleet

NEARCHUS, however, had reached the coast of Carmania safely and had anchored in the harbor of Harmozeia. He sent scouts inland and they met a man who looked like a Greek and who wore Greek clothes. When they addressed him in Greek, he was overjoyed and told them, "I come from Alexander's camp. It is only a few days' march from here." Then the patrol took the Greek to Nearchus. There was great jubilation in the naval camp and Nearchus sent the man back to Alexander posthaste, informing him that he himself would follow in a few days, as soon as the camp was adequately fortified.

When the messenger returned to the army, the joy there was equally great and the envoy was richly rewarded. But day after day passed and Nearchus did not come. Alexander had the messenger flung into chains and he sent out a scouting party with horses and a wagon. Halfway to the sea, they encountered five men who looked like savages. The troop eyed them suspiciously. All the same, they stopped these wretches and questioned them, just in case they had heard anything of Nearchus and the fleet of the Macedonians. "I am Nearchus," said one of the men in rags. "And these are four of my men. Take us to Alexander."

The five climbed into the cart and two of the patrol rode on ahead to the King. "We have found Nearchus and four of his men," they told Alexander. "They are on their way to you." And as they were speaking, the cart drove into the camp. Even Alexander could not tell which of the five men was Nearchus and it was only when the admiral addressed him that Alexander's doubts were removed. He embraced Nearchus and his four companions. "At least you five have been saved, and I thank the gods for it. But tell me, where was the fleet lost?"

"Who speaks of shipwreck?" said Nearchus. "Apart from three ships, the whole fleet is safe in harbor in Harmozeia, five days' march from here."

When Alexander heard this, tears started to his eyes. Once more he embraced Nearchus and said, "This news is worth more to me than all my victories."

Now they all rejoiced and the King feasted the five men at his own table. The messenger who had been put in fetters had his liberty restored and his rewards were doubled.

49

Alexander Receives Nearchus' Account of His Voyage

"AND now, Nearchus, tell us everything that happened," insisted Alexander. And Nearchus told the King and his army all their adventures. He climbed onto a platform so that many people could see him and he told his tale in a loud voice so that everyone could hear.

"As you all know, we were advised to wait on the river Indus until the wind veered and no longer blew from the sea but the land. But our impatience grew with waiting and as soon as there was a lull, we took it as a sign that the wind had changed at last and we rowed out of the river toward the sea. We sailed through a sound with a sprawling island on the left and a rocky shore to the right. Then we found a good harbor and this was fortunate for us, for the wind blew up once more off the sea and kept us stormbound. For four and twenty days we remained in that harbor which we named after Alexander. We had to get water from far inland, for the wells by the coast were all contaminated, and we caught fish and crabs.

"As soon as the wind dropped for the second time, we sailed on to the west. After two days, a gale set in and two galleys and a sailing ship were wrecked against the cliffs. But most of the men who were shipwrecked were able to save themselves, for they were close to the land. When the storm had subsided, we dropped anchor and great was our joy a few days later when we met Leonnatus who had marched toward the coast from the desert with his division. I gave him all the men who had proved to be lazy on board ship and I exchanged them for hard-working soldiers. We sailed on with a fair wind until we reached a bay where we saw a line of warriors drawn up on the shore. They carried wooden spears with tips that had been hardened in the fire. They looked like savages and they were covered all over with hair. As we lowered the boats and rowed toward them, they were frightened by our shining armor and ran away. We captured a few of them. They wore hides and the skins of fishes for clothes, and their miserable huts were built of mud and shells. When they caught fish, they slit them open with knives of stone.

"We had to keep digging wells to find water, for we suffered much from thirst. After a few weeks we came to a coast with palms, myrtles and flowers, where we gathered dates. The natives brought us sheep and fish as gifts, and later they gave us goats as well as baked tunny fish and cakes. And at last we came to a village that had a wall around it.

"These people offered us a pilot. His name was Udraka which means 'fish otter.' He was very resourceful and he knew the places where we would find water. And when we had no more food left, he told us to gather palm shoots and eat them.

"Later we came across a tribe of fisheaters, who do not use boats. They wade into the water at low tide and fish with nets in the pools that the sea leaves behind. Fish provides them with all their sustenance, for they even bake their bread from fish meal.

"We had a great adventure off the coast hereabout. We were sailing over a calm sea beneath a clear sky when suddenly great columns of water spurted up out of the sea directly in our path. The men dropped their oars, they were so startled, and we all feared that the ocean was about to rise against us. Only one person remained calm, and that was our pilot, Udraka. He told us that there are monsters of the deep called whales which are longer than our ships, and it was they who were tossing these trees of water high into the air. He said that the best thing was for us to sail straight at these creatures, which we did. As we charged them we shouted and roared, and when we were near enough to see them, we clanged our swords against our shields and all the trumpeters blew their loudest.

"The rowers smacked the water with the flat of their blades and soon the whales came out of the sea. They lifted their huge skulls above the waves, and when they saw our ships, they became frightened and their tail fins flailed the air. Then they plunged into the deep like sinking ships.

"Behind the fleet, they rose to the surface once more

and, looking back at us, each blew a farewell waterspout. The crews of all our ships burst into wild cheers as if they had won a sea battle and they praised me, their admiral, although they should have given the credit to Fish Otter, our pilot. He had conquered my fear, for he knew more than I did.

"It was on his advice that I changed course from the setting sun to where the Great Bear stands in the sky at night. And thus we came to the coast of Carmania. On our right hand we saw cornfields and meadows, streams and trees, but to the left were the foothills of Makete, where no blade of grass will grow. Then I had an argument with my helmsman, for he wanted to steer south and around these foothills. But I insisted on carrying out my orders, which were to hug the coast and find the shortest route to the Euphrates. And we were rewarded, for soon the harbor of Harmozeia received us. We went ashore and plucked fruit from the trees for it grows there in great abundance. And now I am here."

Then Alexander went to Nearchus and crowned him with a wreath of gold. The soldiers pressed around the admiral and his men. They garlanded them with flowers and ribbons and they carried them shoulder-high through the camp. Never before had a man been given such high honors in Alexander's army.

50

Alexander Punishes the Guilty

THE fleet under Nearchus was now ordered to sail to Susa, while Craterus was to head for the same destination with the main body of the army and the elephants. Craterus had marched from the Indus to Carmania along the great military highway and he had suffered hardly any losses. It was Alexander's intention to celebrate the Macedonian return to Susa with the greatest feast of all time.

He himself would also go to Susa with his cavalry and the light infantry, but by way of Pasagardä, where the tomb of Cyrus stood. Like Alexander, Cyrus had marched through the desert of Gedrosia and, like him too, he had lost his whole army there.

The mausoleum of Cyrus was a simple construction of large stone blocks. It lay hidden among the trees with a spring close by. As Alexander entered the narrow doorway of the tomb, he read this inscription:

> O man, who cometh here, do not grudge me this abode. In it lies Cyrus, son of Cambyses, who founded the Persian Empire and ruled over the whole of Asia.

Vandals had broken into the tomb and robbed the dead king. The golden coffin had been pushed over and the gilded feet chopped off. Rugs, furs dyed purple, necklaces and rings, weapons and ceremonial vessels had all been stolen. Alexander was shocked at the sight of such wanton destruction. The crime could not have been committed long before, and the robbers must have been disturbed in the act, for they had left many things lying on the floor, including the body of the King. The guards had fled for fear of punishment, but Alexander had them tracked down. The grave was restored to all its former glory and placed under the guardianship of the priesthood.

Alexander was in an angry mood as he marched on to Persepolis and there too he found much that was wrong. Satraps who had abused their power were brought before him, and the guilty men were severely punished by the King. One satrap whose crimes had been particularly heinous was made to confess them all before his execution. When he had finished with his recital, Alexander had his say. "Your worst crime you have not even mentioned, so I will tell you what it was. You believed that the desert would engulf me and my army, or you would never have dared to do such evil deeds. And since you behaved as you did, you must have wished for my death and wanted my soldiers to perish too!"

Then the culprit turned pale and Alexander had him led away.

Only one man escaped punishment, and that was Harpalus who had been a boyhood friend of Alexander's. The imperial treasury had been entrusted to his care, but during the Indian campaign Harpalus had led a life of luxury and dissipation in Babylon. Now he fled to Athens with thirty ships, six thousand mercenaries, and all the gold he could lay his hands on, in order to incite the Greeks to rebel against Alexander.

The King chose new satraps from among his followers, one of whom was Peucestas, who had saved Alexander's life in the citadel of the Mallians. He was nominated as a governor and the Persians had a particular affection for him, because he learned their language so quickly.

51

Alexander Holds a Wedding in Susa

IN February the army and the fleet reassembled in Susa. Alexander gave a matchless feast for them all, but first he announced that he would pay off all his soldiers' debts.

During the great expedition nine thousand of his troops had found brides for themselves, and now a mass wedding was to be held. Alexander and his friends took Persian wives as well. Alexander chose two for himself—the eldest daughter of Darius and also a daughter of the previous king, Ochos. Hephaestion married a younger daughter of Darius, for Alexander wanted their children to be cousins. Nearchus, Craterus, Perdiccas, Ptolemy and seventy others married the daughters of the noblest Persian families.

Alexander invited everyone to the marriage feast. Heavy carpets were spread on the ground, under canopies that rested on gilded columns. Eighteen thousand costly chairs were placed in readiness and the bridal couples took their seats upon them, as on thrones, with Alexander and the daughters of the two Great Kings in the middle.

The wedding was celebrated in the Persian fashion, and the festivities went on for five days, with games, contests, music and dancing. And on the last day, when thirty thousand young Persian cadets arrayed in the Macedonian battle dress paraded past the King, the cheering of all the Asian spectators was loud and long.

It was about this time that Alexander received the following letter from Aristotle:

> Aristotle greets the King of the Macedonians and the Greeks and Lord of all Asia. As I hear, you have returned safely from your great campaign. It is no longer fitting for me to advise you what to do, for you have performed a deed greater than any man before you. And he who transcends all others in his supreme qualities is like a god among men, and of the company of those who give the nations their laws.
>
> Nevertheless, I would remind you that you set out on this venture as a Macedonian, acting on behalf of the Greek peoples. You should never forget that the Asians are a different race from us. Be a leader, therefore, for the Macedonians and Greeks, but a master for the barbarians. Cherish the Macedonians and Greeks as you do your own kinsfolk and your friends, but care for the barbarians as for your domestic cattle, which are there to be used. That is my counsel.

The King answered the philosopher thus:

> Alexander greets Aristotle. Your letter greatly surprised me. It is true that Macedonia was my starting point but today I have a far larger fatherland, the whole of the inhabited world. And my kinsmen now are not only Macedonians and Greeks, but all those who can show they are good men. All the rest are barbarians, even if they speak Greek.

This was the letter that Alexander sent to Pella. "Aristotle is too old to understand what it is we are doing," he told Hephaestion.

In Susa the Indian sage, Calanus, fell sick. The desert of Gedrosia had had no ill effect on him, but now he had grown so weak that he could hardly walk.

When he realized that his life was ebbing fast, Calanus decided he would put an end to it in the flames of a funeral pyre. Alexander tried to dissuade him. "Greek doctors will make you well again," he assured the philosopher. Calanus smiled and shook his head. Then a great funeral pyre was built for him, and the entire Macedonian army, except for Alexander, turned out to watch.

Calanus was carried outside on a litter adorned with flowers. He sang a hymn in honor of the gods and divided all his worldly possessions as he took leave of his acquaintances.

The last words he spoke were these: "Be sure to tell Alexander that I shall see him again soon, and it will be in Babylon."

Without any assistance he climbed onto the funeral pyre. His strength seemed to have returned to him. With great dignity he gave the sign for the pyre to be lighted and he remained perfectly calm as the flames surrounded him.

Then all the elephants trumpeted and the soldiers shouted aloud and clanged their spears and shields together, in honor of Calanus.

52

Alexander Quells a Mutiny at Opis

LEAVING Susa, Alexander marched his army up the river Tigris to the city of Opis. There he announced his decision to send the veterans back to Macedonia, and also those who had been wounded—some ten thousand soldiers in all. Every man was to be honored with presents, and Craterus, the first of the generals after Hephaestion, would lead them home.

Alexander expected this announcement to be greeted by a round of applause but instead there was a deathly silence. Dissatisfaction had been mounting in the army since thirty thousand young Persians had been allowed to bear Macedonian arms; and the old campaigners were bitter because their king had made Persians his "kinsfolk."

When Alexander asked his troops why they did not say anything, there were taunts from the ranks that probably he would prefer to send all the Macedonians home so that he could conquer the rest of the world with Persian troops. One voice shouted in scorn, "Go back to your father Ammon!"

For a moment the King seemed paralyzed. The uproar grew and the soldiers pressed forward to the platform on which Alexander stood and they raised their weapons against him.

Alexander was not armed, but he jumped down into the midst of the mutineers, picked out thirteen of those who were shouting the loudest, had them seized by his bodyguard and executed on the spot.

The others were silenced, horror-stricken.

Alexander mounted the rostrum once more. "I shall have nothing more to do with you," he cried, "but I have a few words to say before I leave you. When my father Philip took you into his care, you were beggars, clad in the skins of beasts, and you tended sheep in the mountains. My father gave you cloaks to wear. I have given you Asia. Now you will tell me that you fought bravely and received your share of wounds. I say this to you, 'If there is any man among you who has received more wounds than I, let him step forward.' I have led you to India and I have heaped you with glory. There isn't an army in the world that can hold its own against you—because I have led you from victory to victory. In more than ten years of continuous fighting, not a single soldier of mine has been killed fleeing from the enemy. I have suffered more than anyone. I ate and drank what each of you ate and drank. No one has spared himself less than I have spared myself. But now you want to leave me in the lurch. All right then—do it! Go home to Macedonia and tell them there that you have deserted me. That will bring you great honor. Go!"

Alexander stepped down from the platform and for three days he remained in his palace behind locked doors. Then he called various Persian nobles to him and gave them key appointments. A number of them he elevated and bestowed on them the rank of "Royal Kinsmen." This meant they had the right to greet him with a kiss.

When the Macedonians heard this, they stormed into the palace, threw down their weapons and begged Alexander to forgive them.

Then the King came forth and when he saw their faces

streaming with tears, he was so moved he could not speak. An old soldier raised his voice, "Hey there, our own Alexander! Our minds were confused by evil spirits. But when you make those who are not Macedonians your kinsfolk, it is an insult to the rest of us."

Alexander stretched out his arms. "You are all my kinsfolk from now on!" he cried.

At this they all rushed toward him and those who were near enough kissed him. He invited them to a feast of reconciliation at which ten thousand people of all nationalities sat down together.

53

Alexander Loses Hephaestion and Marches to Babylon

SOON after these events, Alexander received a blow from which he never quite recovered. Hephaestion died. They had to use force to drag the King away from the body of his friend.

Alexander had Hephaestion's remains taken to Babylon and there a superb tomb was built for him. Messengers were sent to consult the oracle in the desert. They were to find out if the gods had taken Hephaestion to a place where Alexander would be united with him again after death.

The brigade that Hephaestion had led was not given a new general. Alexander allowed it to keep its old name, and he commanded it personally. Then he set off for Babylon to carry out the funeral rites for the dead man, and to make preparations for another great expedition. This was designed to conquer all the western lands.

As Alexander approached Babylon, the wise men of the Chaldaeans came out of the town to meet him. They insisted on speaking to the King alone and when everyone else had been dismissed, they said, "We have learned through our god that evil will come upon you if you enter Babylon. Great danger awaits you there."

Alexander thanked the seers for their consideration, but this was his reply: "Wise men that you are, you must know that it is impossible for me to turn my back on danger."

Defying all the portents, he marched on. He refused to be put off even when a flock of ravens overhead attacked a big shining bird. They savaged it so cruelly that it fell to the ground immediately in front of Alexander's horse, so that it shied in fright. Alexander spurred his steed on and entered Babylon.

There, indeed, something occurred that gave him food for thought. He was playing ball with his friends and, as was his custom, he had stripped for the game. When he went to put on his clothes again, they could not be found. Then an officer of his bodyguard came hurrying straight from the palace, and he announced that a stranger was sitting on the throne, clad in the King's garments and wearing the royal diadem.

Alexander and his friends hastened into the throne room. The stranger sat silent on the throne, staring into space. It was only after many questions were put to him that he spoke at last. "My name is Dionysus, and I come from the coast. I was being held in prison, but the god Serapis removed my fetters and bade me to take Alexander's clothes and his coronet and sit upon his throne."

Alexander had the man removed and the clothes were burned. And he remembered the words of the Indian sage who, before he died, had promised he would see him again in Babylon.

During the following weeks, Alexander received ambassadors from the west. From Africa there came Libyans and Ethiopians; from Italy Lucanians, Bruttians and Etruscans. From the far west there came Iberians and Celts, for Alexander's fame had reached them too. They were astonished to hear of his new plans, how he intended to travel around Arabia and Africa and thus approach the Pillars of Herakles from the west. Work had already begun on a new harbor south of Babylon, which would be big enough to take one thousand ships. In May Alexander sailed down the Euphrates, in order to found another city at the mouth, the twelfth to bear his name. This would be the starting point for the great expedition to the west.

When he was back in Babylon, the King sat feasting with his friends. No one was gayer than Alexander that night, but suddenly he was seized with a violent fever.

The nights were sultry, the days unbearably hot. Alexander told his servants to carry him out of his palace on the west bank of the river, and into the royal gardens. In the shade of an old tree he received Nearchus and the other generals, to give them his last instructions for the western enterprise.

Day by day the fever increased. From his sick bed Alexander sacrificed to the gods ceaselessly and issued commands concerning the new expedition.

Toward the end Alexander found it more and more difficult to talk. His words grew delirious. He asked for water from the oasis as if he were already in the Arabian desert. His Companions stood around him in deep silence. And they feared for the life of their king.

54

Alexander Ranges the Skies and the Seas in His Delirium

ALEXANDER saw Arabia lying beneath him. He could see as far as the Red Sea, for he was standing on top of a high mountain. Around him were his closest friends, among them Hephaestion and Cleitus. From the height of the peak, the sky did not seem far away. And Alexander said, "Bring me a ladder so that I can mount to the sky and touch it with my hand. I wish to find out if it is made of burnished metal, or if it is a flowing stream of light."

The ladder was brought, and Alexander saw at once that he could not reach the sky with it. But his desire to do so was so strong that he made the mountain move, and a crack opened up in the rock, out of which came two griffins with mighty wings. They were harnessed to a chariot that was nothing but a golden armchair. Alexander sat down in it and he grasped the air with such strength that the rays of the sun became a spear in his hand. On the tip of this spear Alexander spiked a lump of meat, and as the griffins were greedy for the carrion, Alexander dangled it above their heads. The beasts flew upward in an effort to reach the food and thus did Alexander drive his chariot. The griffins flew so high that Alexander could see the whole earth stretched out below him. It lay like a round island set in a bottomless sea.

High in the sky, Alexander was overwhelmed with a new longing, this time to plumb the depths of the ocean, so he lowered the bait and held it out below the feet of the griffins. Thus he steered them back to the mountain where his friends were waiting for him.

They were glad when he was back in their midst once again, but all he said was "Now we shall put to sea and sail our ship to the place where the ocean is deepest."

And although his friends tried urgently to dissuade him, he had himself enclosed in a glass barrel and lowered into the sea at the end of a long rope. There he saw fishes that no one had ever seen before, because they never leave the depths of the sea and fear the light of the sun. They carry lights of their own, either fixed to their foreheads or on their backs. They swam past the glass barrel and were startled at the sight of it. Giant crabs and octopuses with tentacles as long as spears came toward him, but they too fled when they saw Alexander, and retreated into the darkness where the sea is deepest.

Then Alexander had the barrel hauled up to the ship again, so that he would not be alone any longer.

When the King opened his eyes once more, his expression revealed that he had returned from a great distance, and he gazed at his friends standing around his couch—Perdiccas and Ptolemy, Leonnatus and Peucestas, Craterus, Seleucus and Nearchus.

The army was waiting outside the palace. Alexander made a sign toward the entrance. Then Perdiccas had the gates flung wide open and the soldiers filed past to see their king again.

When the procession was over, Alexander gave his signet ring to Perdiccas.

As night fell, Seleucus and Peucestas went up to the shrine of Serapis. There they kept vigil all night long, in order to learn from the god if it would be a good thing to carry the King into the sanctuary. The next morning they learned the god's answer from the priests: they should leave the King where he was. That was best for him.

When Seleucus and Peucestas returned to the royal palace, Alexander was dead.

55

Alexander's Legacy Begins a Great Quarrel

A GREAT lamentation arose in the town of Babylon, and the news of Alexander's death spread quickly throughout the lands. When Sisygambis, the mother of Darius, heard of it in her palace at Susa, her grief was so great that she pined away and died of sorrow.

Perdiccas, who had received Alexander's signet ring, called the army together to choose a new king. A throne was set up in front of the palace, and on it Perdiccas placed the ring, as a sign that he too would submit to the will of the army. But in his heart he felt sure that the army would proclaim him king.

The other generals thought likewise, for now that Alexander was dead, each believed that he was the best man to succeed the King.

But the army failed to come to a decision. The soldiers did not consider that any of those who were casting eyes on the crown were worthy of taking Alexander's place.

Then the generals told the soldiers to go back to their camp, and they conferred among themselves.

"It is up to us to choose one of our number," proposed Peucestas. "If we can agree among ourselves, the army will approve our choice."

"First we must decide what is to be done," said Perdiccas.

"There's no argument about that," said Nearchus. "Alexander wanted to unite the east and the west. Everything is ready for the great march to the west."

"Another grand expedition!" jeered Seleucus. "Isn't the empire big enough already?"

"What about the thousand ships that Alexander has built? Are they to be burned then?" asked Nearchus angrily.

"Sail them to the Pillars of Herakles yourself then," Seleucus dared him. "Or is there anyone else here who is willing to take part in this campaign?"

No one spoke.

"You see!" said Seleucus to Nearchus. "The rest of us are of one mind—the empire is big enough already."

"It is too big for one person . . ." Ptolemy began.

"What do you mean by that?" Perdiccas interrupted him.

"That we should divide it up between us," said Ptolemy. "Why should only one of us be king? Are we not equals?"

Then Perdiccas spoke up. "Alexander gave me his signet ring."

"That was another of his mistakes," said Craterus brusquely.

"This is no time to speak of Alexander's mistakes," Nearchus defended his late king.

"We must speak of them," protested Seleucus hotly, "so that we do not repeat them ourselves."

"He is right," said Ptolemy. "It was a mistake to march to the end of the world instead of conquering only as much as a man can rule. Above all, it was a mistake to remove the differences between the conquerors and the conquered. Alexander had become an Asian himself and he has made us half-Asians too. Nothing is more necessary than to remind ourselves that we are Macedonians. The rest, on the other hand, are subject peoples and they must obey us."

"What you are saying contradicts everything that Alexander stood for," said Nearchus. "He would have rebuked you for those words."

"Alexander is dead," said Craterus in a hard voice. "We are alive and it is we who have to act."

"You are betraying him!" cried Nearchus in wrath.

"We have done only what he considered right for long enough," said Craterus. "At last we are free."

Nearchus looked from one to the other and they made no secret of the fact that they all shared Craterus' opinion. Then Nearchus got up and left. When he had gone, the others began quarreling anew. They argued so violently that the palace courtyard echoed with the uproar, and they wrangled until far into the night.

In the end, they carved up Alexander's empire so that each was satisfied with his share for the moment. Each of them seized a throne for himself and called himself a king. But soon they were quarreling again. They envied each other

126

villages and towns, islands and whole provinces. Presently the arguments were no longer confined to words but were continued with the sword. More people lost their lives in these conflicts than on the great march to India. And the nations who became embroiled in one war after another mourned for Alexander.

HEREWITH ends my account of Alexander's great expedition.

I am told that there was even a dispute as to where Alexander should be buried. In the end, Ptolemy, who became Pharaoh of Egypt, took the body of the dead king with him and he buried it in the city which Alexander founded at the mouth of the Nile and which he had honored with his name. From there, so they say, the corpse was secretly transported to the oasis of Siwah in the desert, but no one knows for certain, not even I, the King's Runner and Pace-recorder of Asia. For I did not go with him on this, his second journey into the desert. I went home.

On the long march back from Babylon to Macedonia, I was often questioned about Alexander. Everyone envied me for having gone with him, and I cannot regret that I marched with him to India for he gave us all the opportunity to marvel at the man and his deeds.

Alexander did not inspire my love, I admit it freely. I gave that to others I met on the great campaign; to Porus, the conquered king, and to Taxiles, who rode to meet Alexander alone and unarmed, and who stretched out his hand in friendship. It seemed to me that the greatest of all the kings I saw was Dindimus, who sent his soldiers home so that they could till their fields.

Nearer to my heart too was Nearchus the Cretan, and I admired most the philosopher Callisthenes, who remained standing before the King when all the rest knelt, and who spoke his mind fearlessly.

I discovered many things in Alexander which shocked me. But I saw too that he was capable of repentance when he had let his passions overrule him and drive him to commit an evil deed. He, the invincible, conquered himself on the banks of the Hyphasis, when he realized that his men had come to the end of their strength. And when he removed the distinctions between the conquerors and the conquered, when he reconciled the nations in spite of the opposition of his own people, then one can truly call him a great man who has few peers even among the mighty.

As one of the pacers who marched with Alexander, that is what I think.

B.C. 356 Alexander born in Pella, Macedonia.

344 Aristotle appointed Alexander's tutor.

340 Philip names Alexander as Regent during his campaign against Byzantium.

339 Alexander defeats the Thracians.

338 Alexander commands the Macedonian cavalry at the Battle of Chaeronea.

337 Alexander goes into exile with his mother; King Philip's second marriage, to the young princess, Cleopatra.

336 Philip assassinated; Alexander acclaimed King of Macedonia; Darius III becomes Great King of Asia.

335 Alexander marches to the Danube and into Illyria; the destruction of Thebes.

334 The Great Expedition into Asia is launched; Alexander crosses the Hellespont in the spring and wins the Battle of Granicus.

333 The Macedonian army invades Cilicia; Alexander ill after bathing in the Cydnus; wins the Battle of Issus in November.

332 Tyre conquered after a seven months' siege, Gaza after a siege of two months; Alexander advances into Egypt and visits the oasis of Siwah; he founds Alexandria and orders the exploration of the Nile.

331 The Macedonian army sets out for Phoenicia in

the spring and crosses the Euphrates in July; on October 1, Alexander wins the Battle of Gaugamela and enters Babylon.

330 Alexander enters Persepolis and pursues Darius, who is assassinated in July; the army fights in Hyrcania, Aria and Drangiana; Philotas and others executed following a conspiracy and Parmenion murdered.

329 Alexander crosses the Hindu Kush in the spring and invades Bactria and Sogdiana; Bessus handed over; the Macedonians conquer the Scythians and set up winter quarters in Bactria.

328 Hard fighting in Sogdiana; Alexander marries Roxana, the daughter of Ariamazes; Cleitus, appointed Governor of Bactria and Sogdiana, is killed by Alexander at a feast in his honor.

327 Alexander's army sets off for India, and sets up winter quarters by the upper Indus.

326 Alexander marches into Taxila, crosses the Hydaspes, defeats Porus and proceeds to the Hyphasis; the army forces him to turn back; Alexander has a fleet built and sails down the Hydaspes; the army conquers Mallian towns and spends the winter in the kingdom of Musicanus.

325 Alexander sails down a branch of the Indus into the Indian Ocean; in his march through the Gedrosian Desert, ninety thousand of his followers die; Nearchus sails with the fleet to the Persian Gulf.

324 In Persepolis, Alexander punishes corrupt satraps; the mass wedding of nine thousand Macedonians to Asian brides takes place in Susa; Alexander

marries daughters of two Great Kings, Darius and Ochos; he quells a mutiny of the Macedonian army in Opis.

323 Alexander goes to Babylon, makes preparations for an expedition to the west and the circumnavigation of Africa; death of Alexander, June 11 (or 13); his empire disintegrates overnight; bitter struggles for many years among his successors; the great expedition, however, continues to influence all spheres of human activity—down to the present day.